AF449257

HARD KNOCKS

Rolling with the Derby Girls

Shelley Calton

HARD KNOCKS

Rolling with the Derby Girls

KEHRER

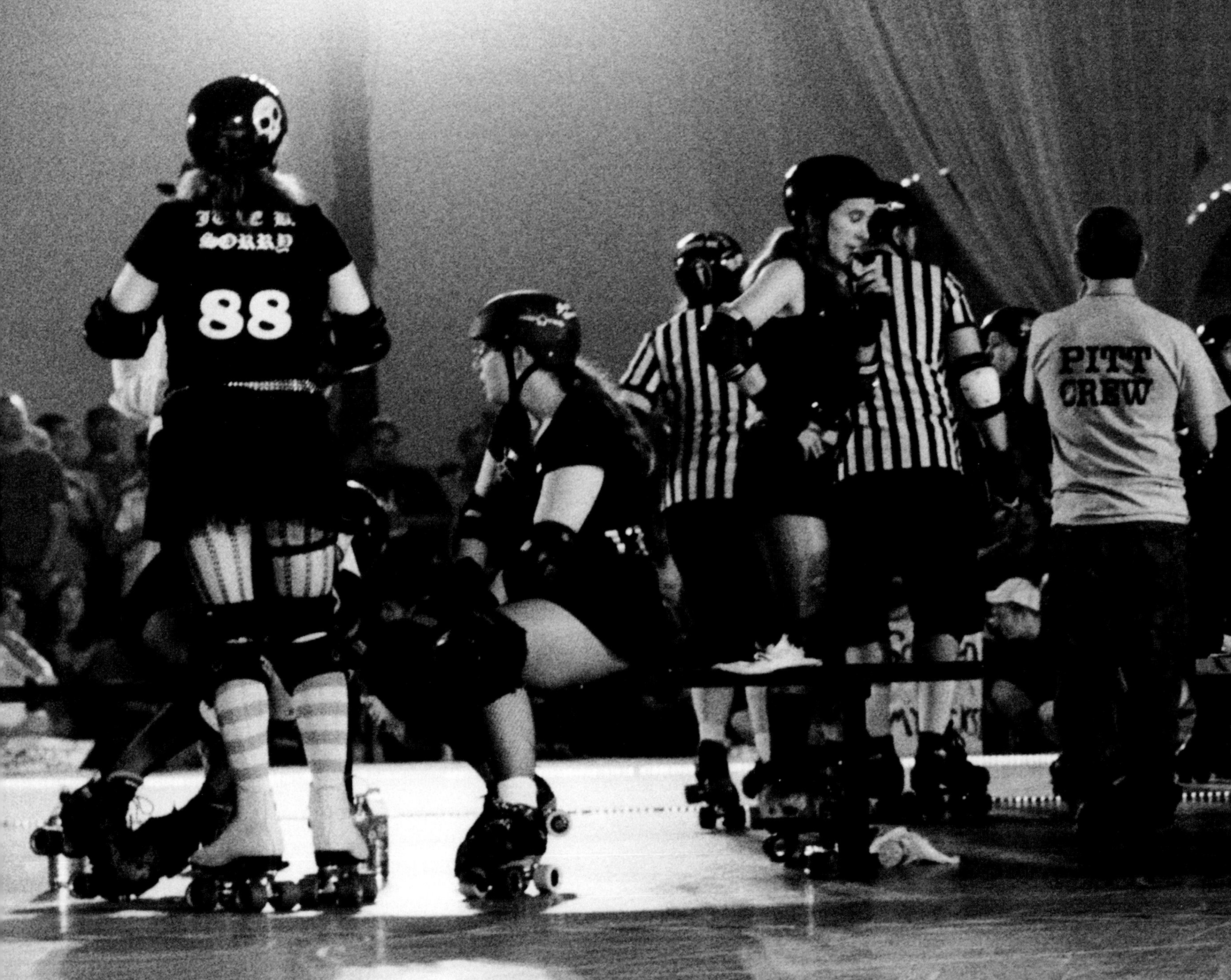

JUL B.
SORRY
88
PITT
CREW

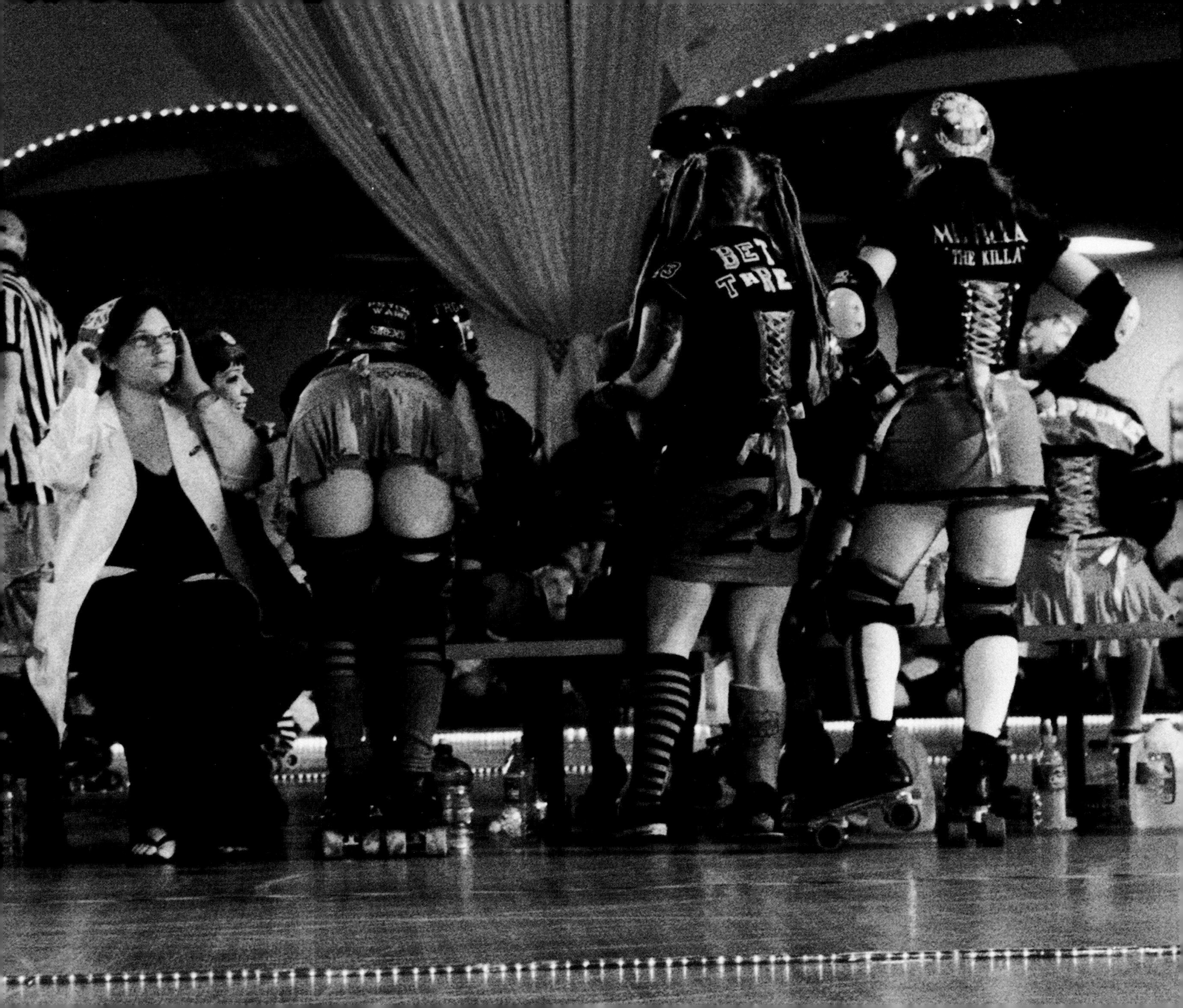

BET
TAPE
MILLA
"THE KILLA"

To the women, whose strength I draw from, the women of the Houston Roller Derby.

STATE MENT

Rolling with the Derby Girls

When I initially immersed myself into the world of Roller Derby, I believed it was only about the grass roots revival of a women's contact team sport. I soon discovered that Derby is really about empowered women breaking barriers and creating new boundaries. I developed a great deal of respect for these women, as well as envy, and I wish I had the courage to skate with them. Without getting paid and constantly running the risk of serious injury, these women transform themselves from moms, teachers, and business women into competitive athletes. The Derby names they give themselves reveal a bit about them individually *i.e.*, "Tawdry Hepburn" and "Patsy Crime." Through my photographs, I endeavor to capture the femininity, diversity, spirit, and strength of the women of Roller Derby.

Shelley Calton

FORE WORD

Dualities of Gender and Transformation
By Tracy Xavia Karner

Shelley Calton photographs at the intersection of gender and sport. In her arresting and highly energetic series *Hard Knocks*, Calton immerses herself in the intense action of the Houston Roller Derby, following the skaters closely as they confront, disrupt and, ultimately, subvert traditional gender expectations. Female contact team sports are so uncommon that we have pre-conceptions of how women might act and what they might look like while engaged in competitive "play." With tenacious documentary skill and unmistakable romantic verve, Calton captures the nascent phase of this new form of "femininity, diversity, spirit and strength," photographing the women as they redefine both the game and themselves. Using a medium-format film camera, Calton suspends the women and the sport in a cinematic-style gaze cloaked with a nostalgic black and white, grainy *film noir* tonality that frames the action in historical context, referencing the departure of the new from the old. Thinking back to the late-night, 3:4 rectangle of the black and white television screen, today's skaters surface from a history of sport which had previously been co-ed and achieved its highest popularity in the 1950s.

Calton, a native Houstonian and a skater in her youth, started photographing the Houston Roller Derby during their initial practice sessions in 2005. Mesmerized by the fast-paced skaters whirling around the track with raucous in-your-face sexuality, Calton found "role models" of empowered women testing their skills, honing their strengths, and competing aggressively. The sharply observed images in *Hard Knocks* appear firmly rooted in the traditions of social documentary photography, which illuminates the close affinity between the humanity of the photographer and the experiences of the subjects. This is perhaps epitomized in *Applying Lipstick, 2005*, as Calton shows how familiar female tropes like lipstick and irons, traditional symbols of previous female oppression and gender inequity, can be refashioned as props for a new kind of feminine performance. What emerges from Calton's sensitive study is a duality of gender in transition – the female photographer and the women skaters – played out within the frame. Her stylistic *noir*, perfected in previous work (Dreams of Geppetto and Escape) finds full expression in this series.

Claiming Keith Carter and Debbie Fleming Cafferty as her early inspirations, Calton extracts the evocative unknown of these young women and their transitional lives through her focus on the duality of their performances – their individual vulnerability that slips out from behind alter ego costumes. Light streams down illuminating only a glimpse of the waiting performer in *Psycho Billie, 2005*, a pensive tranquility in her face as she waits to enter the rink. Calton's admiration and appreciation for the women she photographs is evidenced in the detail and craft of each print. Immersed in the tactile process of traditional photography, Calton makes her own gelatin silver prints which are then selenium-toned for aesthetic as well as archival purposes, adding to their sense of depth and richness. There is an intrinsic symmetry in Calton's own transformation into documentary work about women resurrecting and reconfiguring an all but forgotten sport. Her previous photographic work was in controlled and constructed environments – quite different from the action-packed arena of the Roller Derby.

In terms of its demands, the exertion, skill, and showmanship required, the new all-female Roller Derby has been compared to the traditionally male sports of football or wrestling.

Invented by Leo Seltzer in 1930s Chicago, Roller Derby was originally a co-ed sport that went through various phases of popularity. Contemporary all-female Roller Derby – the Houston Roller Derby being one example – has a new attitude of aggressive competition, spirited hyjinx, sexuality, brawls, bruises and drama. Originating in 2001 in Austin, Texas, an imaginative, lively group put together their own DIY (do-it-yourself), skater-owned league ("By the skaters, for the skaters") that has inspired more than 130 similar leagues all around the United States. Roller Derby bouts (games) consist of two twenty-minute periods where two teams of five skaters are on the track. Each team has three blockers, a pivot, and a jammer. Blockers clear the path for the jammer, who scores team points by passing the opponent blockers or the pivot. The pivot sets the pace of the "jam" (play) and blocks as well.

The bouts of the first season were held in the Arabia Shrine
Temple with its luxurious crystal chandeliers and sweeping satin
curtains, providing a visually striking backdrop, and an amusing
contrast to the quad skates, risqué costumes, and sweaty athletes.
Set within such a perfect theatrical venue, the cinematic narrative
unfolds image by image providing a glimpse into this seemingly
transgressive community. *The Rink, 2006* sets the tenor for our
viewing; we look down on the action as if in the opening scene of
an old movie. The crystal chandelier glistens with lavish formal-
ity above the energetic swirl of skaters forming their initial lineup.
In the cavernous space the light is uneven, and the shadows exag-
gerated as we are introduced to this spectacle. One expects the
camera to pan closer, zooming from overhead, in a single shot
bringing us intimately into the fray. Calton astutely plays on this
desire, and perceptively positions viewers as voyeurs. We observe
private moments in the dressing room, witness erotic warm-ups,
watch as injuries are iced. We see Elle McFierce stretching, Agent
Belligerent tightening her wheels, Tex Offender packing pistols,
Vanna Whitetrash fixing her hair, Flame & Rage jamming,
Dolly Le Dukes lacing her skates, and Hardcora limping.

Indeed we are beguiled by the spectacle, hopelessly smitten with the possibility of joy and novelty. In sequined bustier, arms in the air, Patsy Crime *(Patsy Crime, 2006)* positively exudes delight and triumph in her new-found role. There is a carnival atmosphere as the announcers circle the track in costume. The Colonel, in his tan leisure suit with cowboy hat and boots, dances, runs, and drinks pickle juice; Cap'n Jack Sorrow in full pirate garb; Penalty Mistresses Monsta and Malice dressed in matching ruffled short skirts; even the referees in costume – it is a circus with one ring. We have peeked out from behind the curtains of gender norms to discover a femininity that manifests exuberance without apology; and we are captivated. There is nothing tame or measured in the Roller Derby. It is a high-energy sport. Loud, fast-paced music plays on track-side speakers during the game – it is a party with skaters at the center. The women in fishnet stockings and bustiers fly around the track with quads spinning. Bodies collide in competition and elation. Looks are exchanged, plays are executed, and points are won. Calton's *film noir* aesthetic distills but obscures the edges between life on and off the track.

We are drawn in by this murky nostalgic gaze as it illuminates new possibilities for competition and sisterhood. Flame & Rage in lead jammer position, the Colonel with his arms outstretched, and the Penalty Mistresses Monsta and Malice sharing a knowing glance all call to mind the movie posters of the 1950s. *EXCITEMENT! SCREAMS! FEEL* the unbridled passion! *SEE* the hottest women on wheels! Women who skate symbolically rename themselves to establish their Derby personas – Death by Chocolate, The Prosecuter, disMae West, Carmen Gedit, Holla Pain Yo, Kerrizma Kevorkian, Chewcifer, Flame & Rage – and individualize their team costume to suit their new selves. The uniforms are bold and flashy, designed for maximum movement with minimum fabric. Fishnets, torn t-shirts, boisterous sexuality, showgirl makeup, and lingerie predominate. With remarkable sensitivity, Calton captures the duality of the women and their skaters' alter egos in compelling and evocative portraits. Taken in available light and just before the women enter the track to skate in a bout, they express the liminal space between the private backstage and public frontstage of their skater performance.

The large-format Graflex camera with Polaroid type 55 film accentuates the gritty determination of an athlete in that pensive moment, revealed in seductive half light, before taking center stage. In *Agent Belligerent, 2006* we see her costumed and ready, yet somehow conveying deep vulnerability as she looks into the camera. Kerrizma Kevorkian's soulful eyes *(Kerrizma Kevorkian, 2006)* meet the camera's gaze with disarming and intense innocence. Calton's portraits are transfixing and enthralling, effectively revealing the women behind the performances.

Shelley Calton's *Hard Knocks* invites us into this energetic realm of dedicated yet playful, competitive yet supportive, retro yet progressive women. Through Calton's images, we see gender sensibilities subverted, inverted and remade into new, more inventive and fully realized identities. This work suggests possibilities for all of us.

Tracy Xavia Karner
Director of Visual Studies,
Associate Professor of Sociology,
University of Houston

ACKNOWLEDGMENTS

from Shelley Calton

I dedicate this book to the Women of the Houston Roller Derby, who accepted me and allowed me the freedom to capture their spirit and soul. A special thank you to skaters Dana Beck and Chrissy Grove for your help and inspiration.

Many thanks go to my friends, family, and loved ones. My sisters Kelly, Shannon, and Janice; my nieces Taylor and Lexi; and my parents, Allen and Lil. To Larry Coyle for your love and unwavering support throughout my craziness. My deepest gratitude to John Spellos and Nanci Calton for your friendship and advice throughout the years. My sincerest appreciation to Dennis Calton, Madeline Yale, Bevin Bering, Kathryn Urbanek, and Raul Marroquin for your encouragement and support. I am forever indebted to my friends and mentors, Keith Carter and Debbie Fleming Caffery. Your guidance is invaluable. Thank you to Tracy Karner for your beautifully written essay. My gratitude to Leslie Jean Stuart for her beautiful book design, for taking my dreams and making them a reality on paper. Also, thanks to Alexa Becker and Klaus Kehrer for your leap of faith in making this project a book.

"Bonding with all of the women, I feel like they are my sisters."

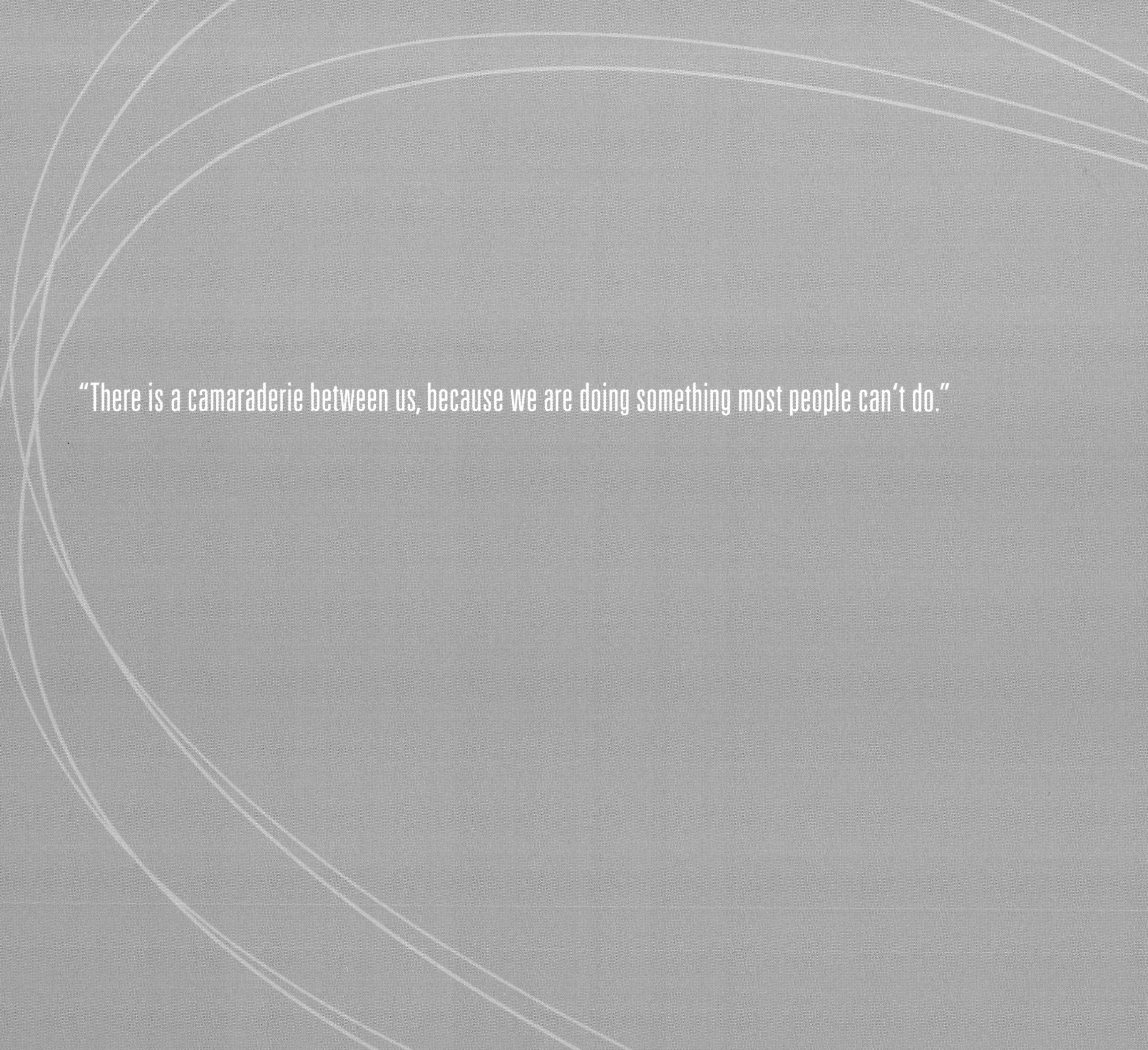

"There is a camaraderie between us, because we are doing something most people can't do."

"Winning is everything. I don't go out there to do anything else but win."

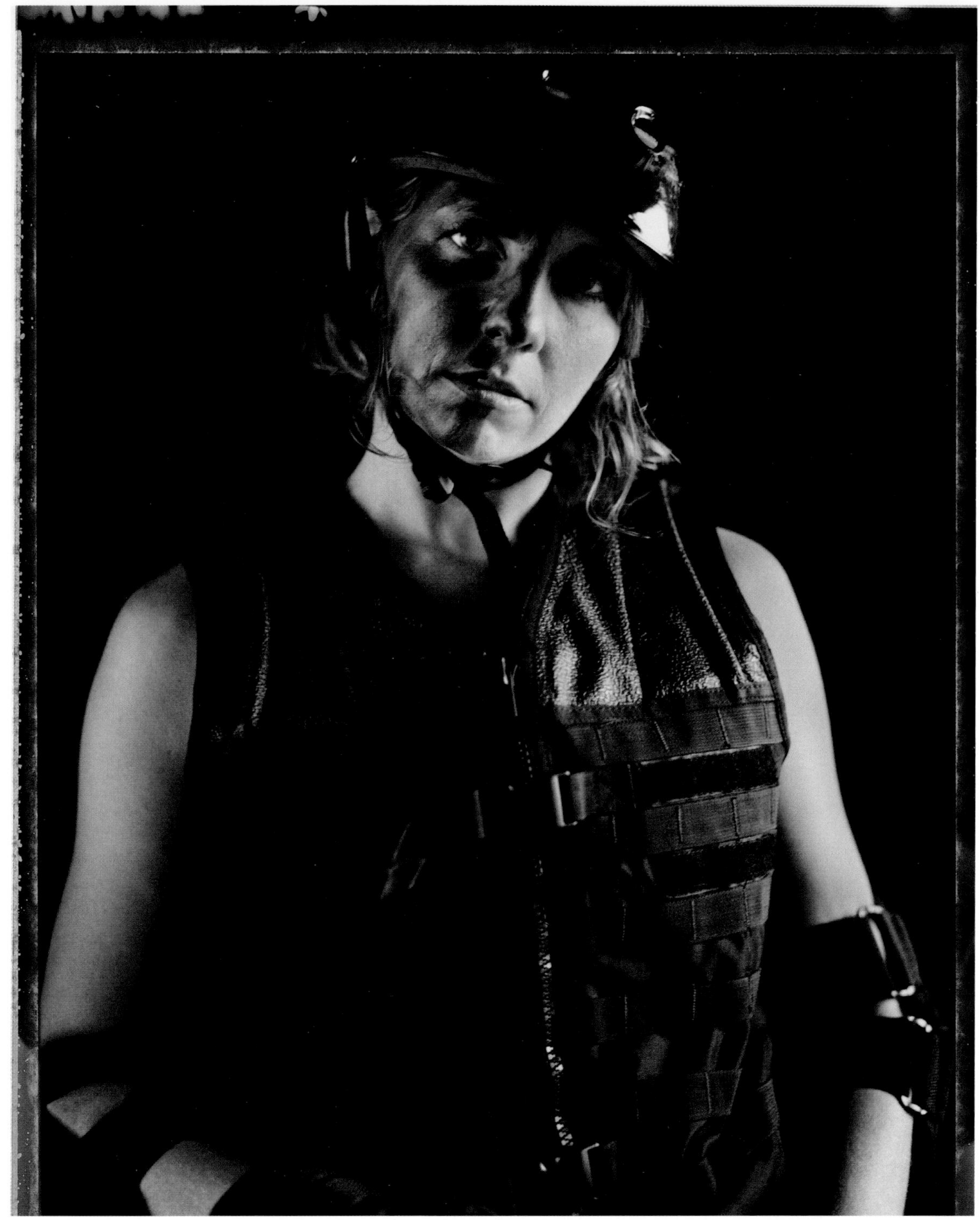

Agent Belligerent

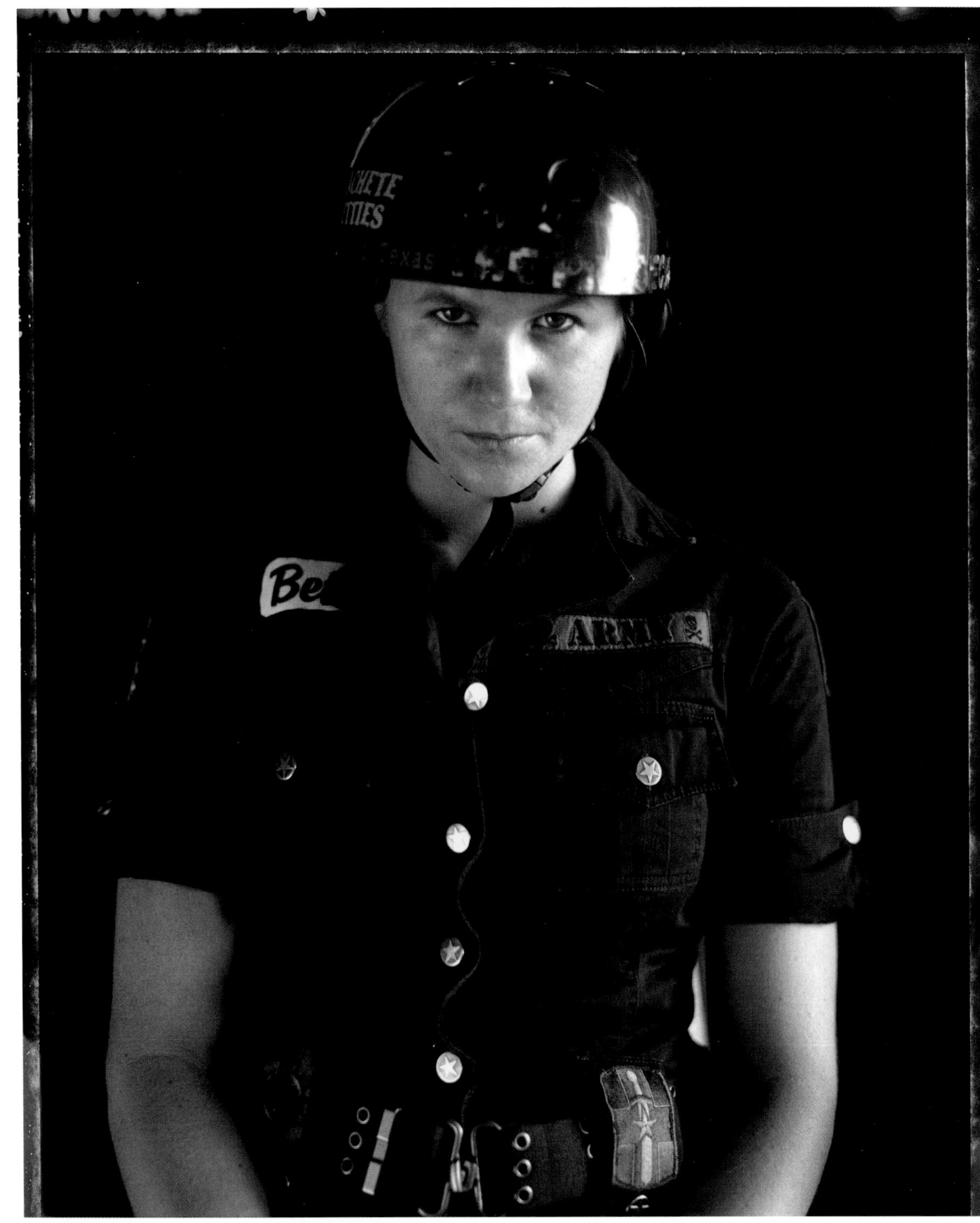

The Prosecutor

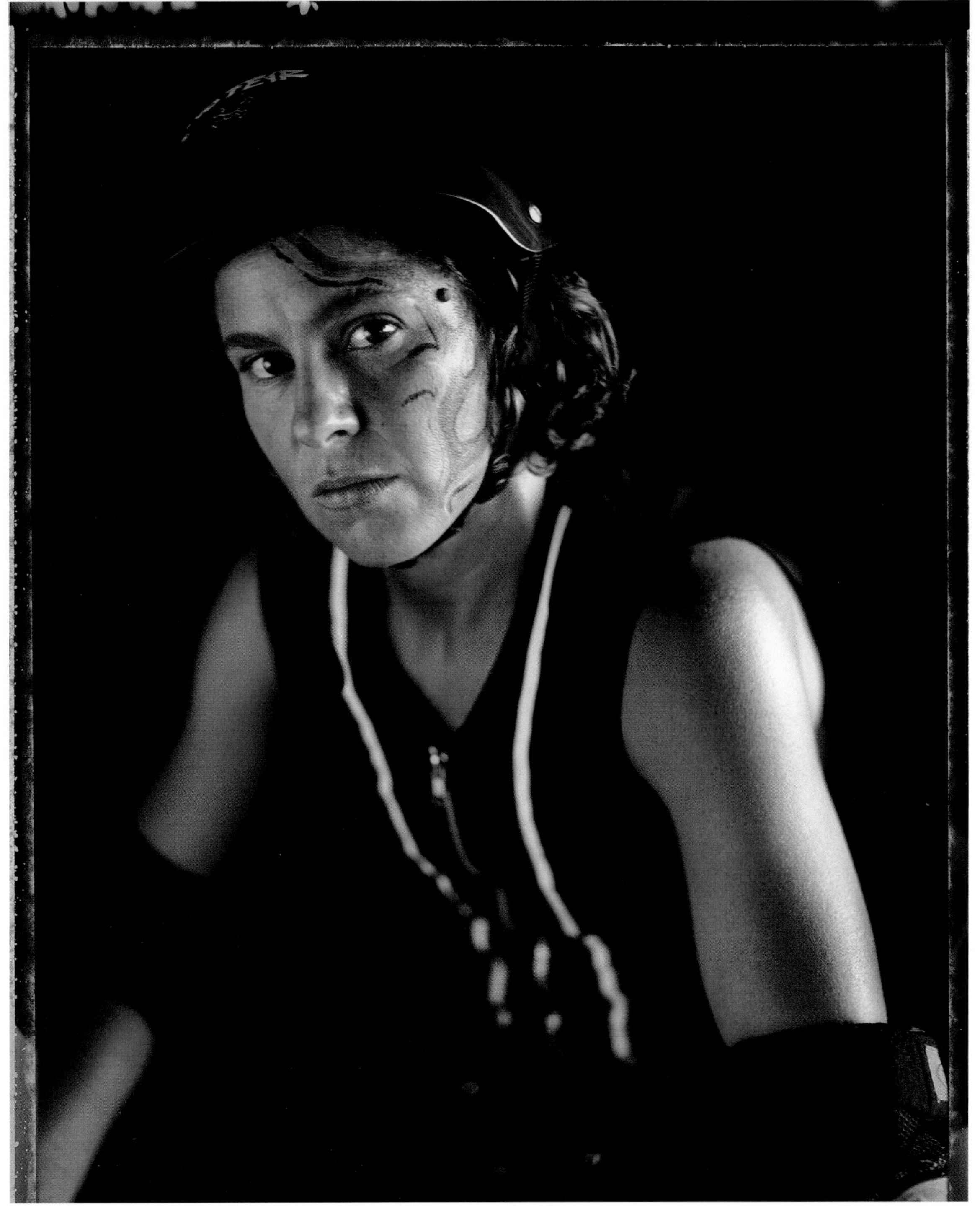

Flame & Rage

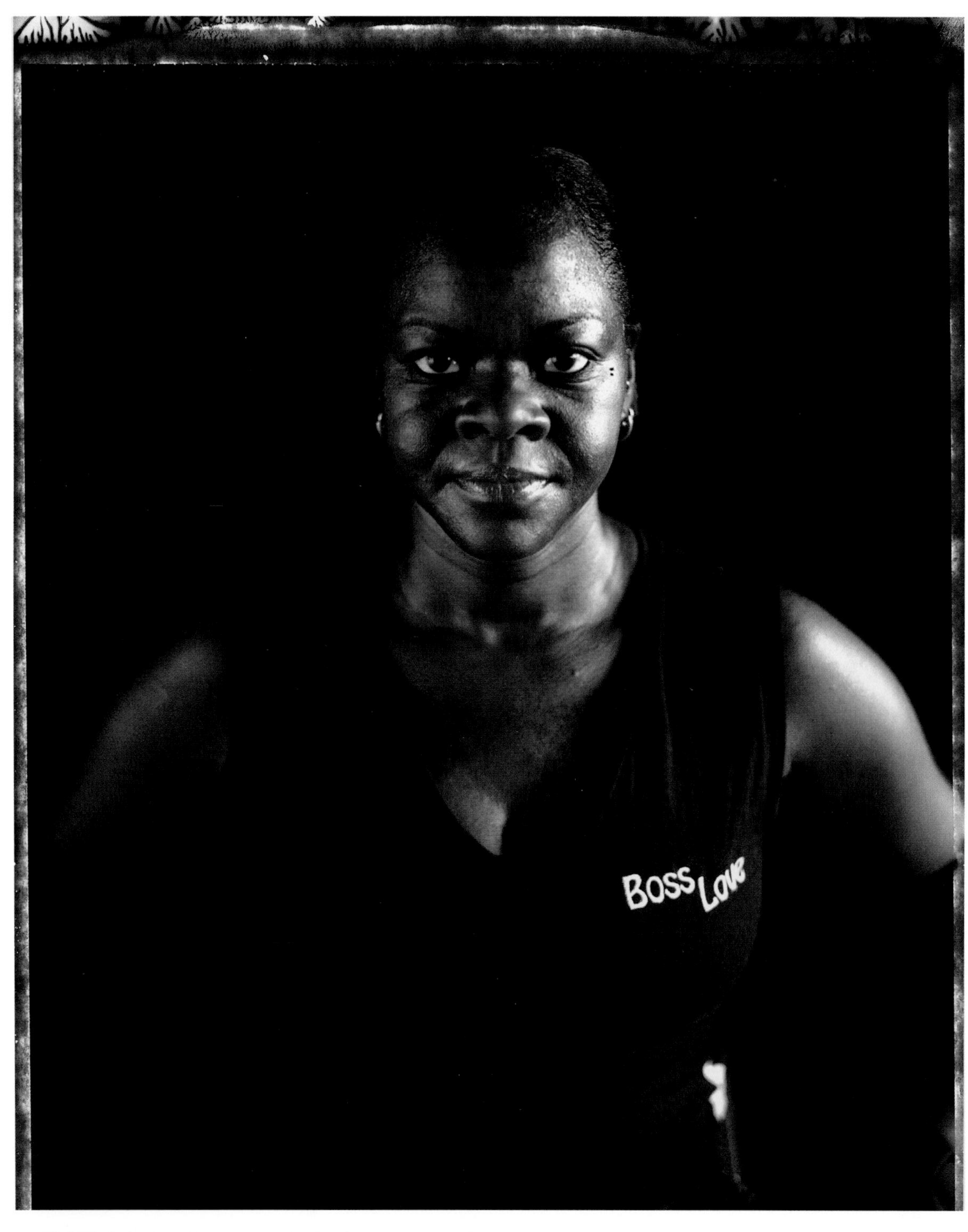

Death by Chocolate

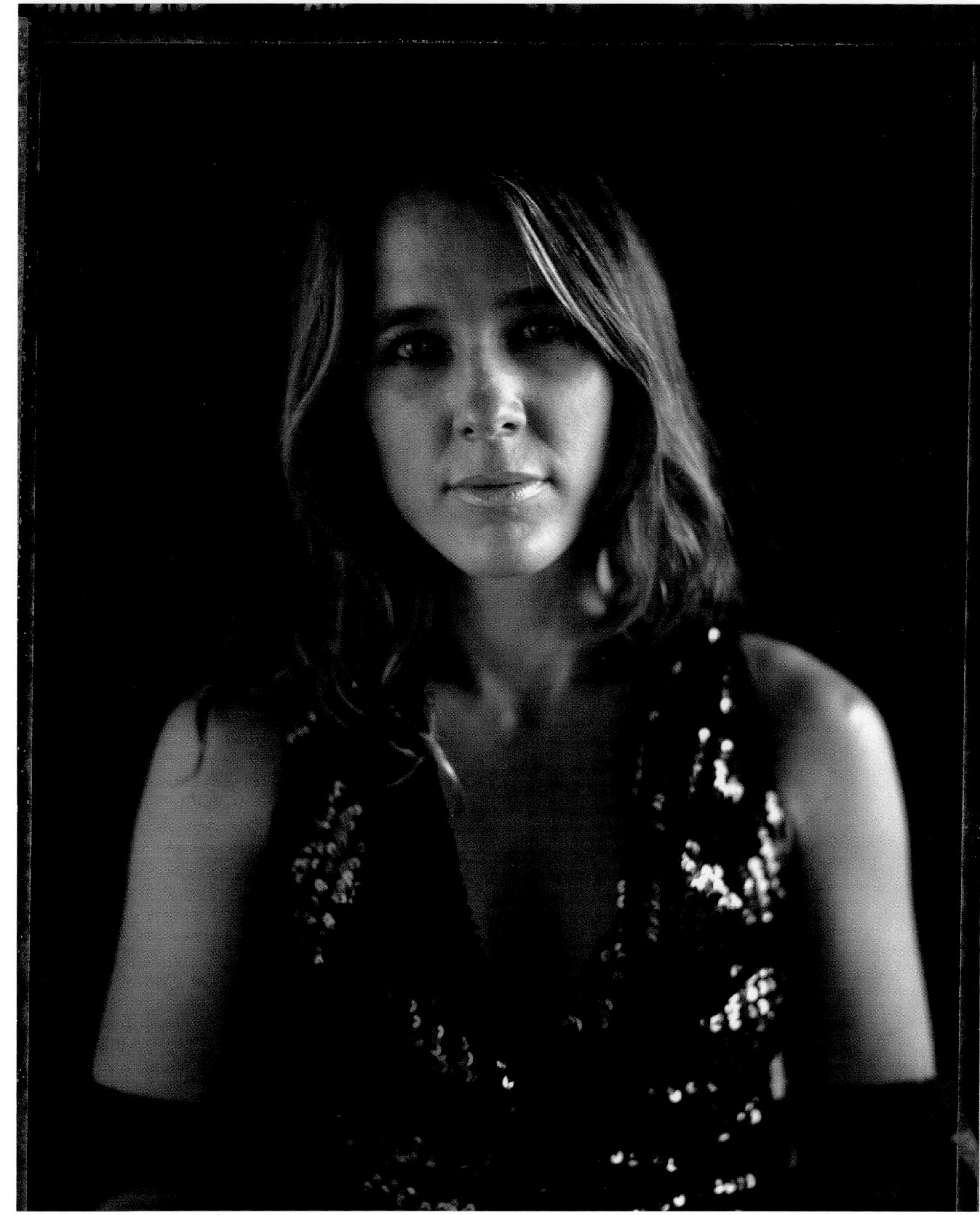

Holla pain yo

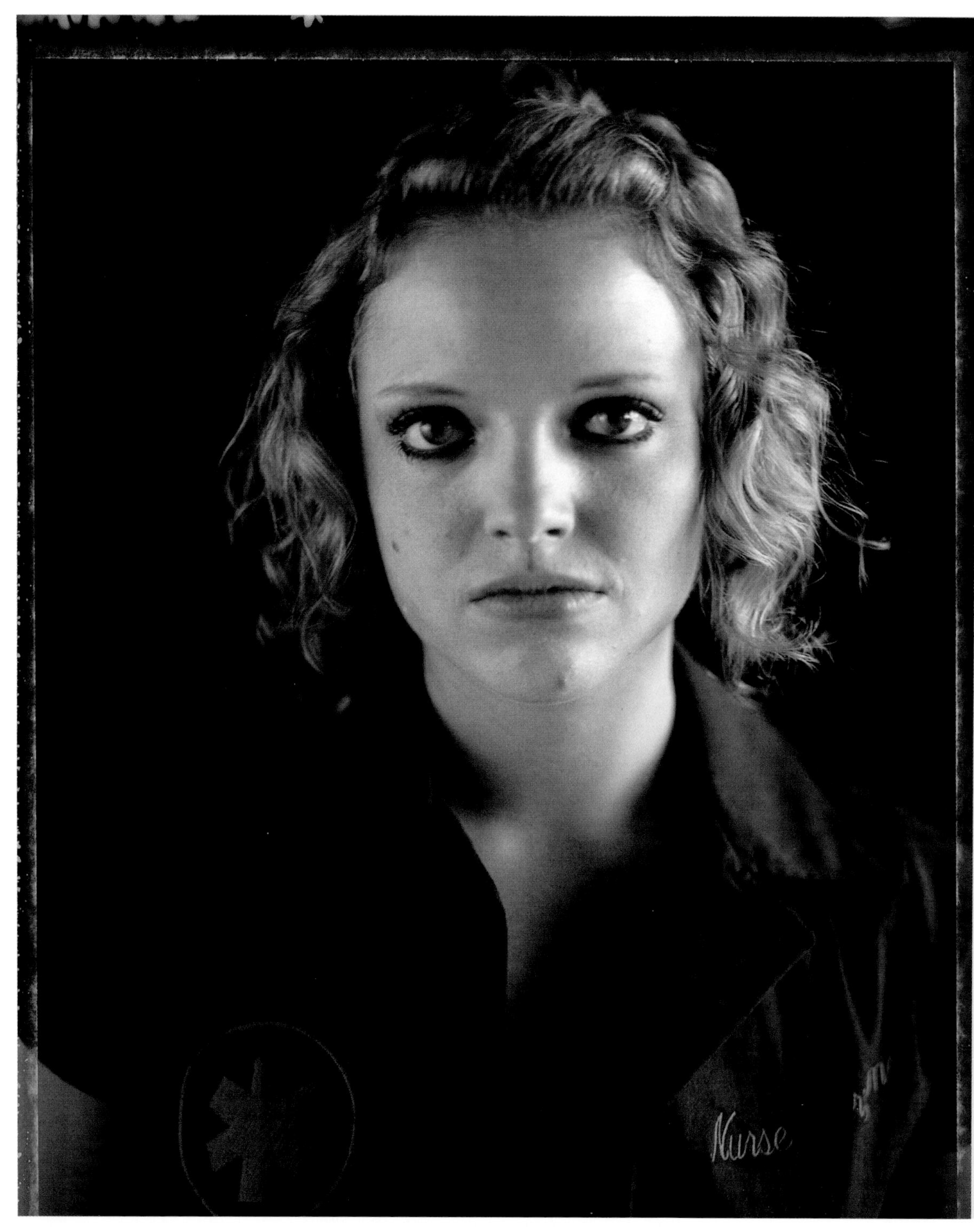

Kerrizma Kevorkian

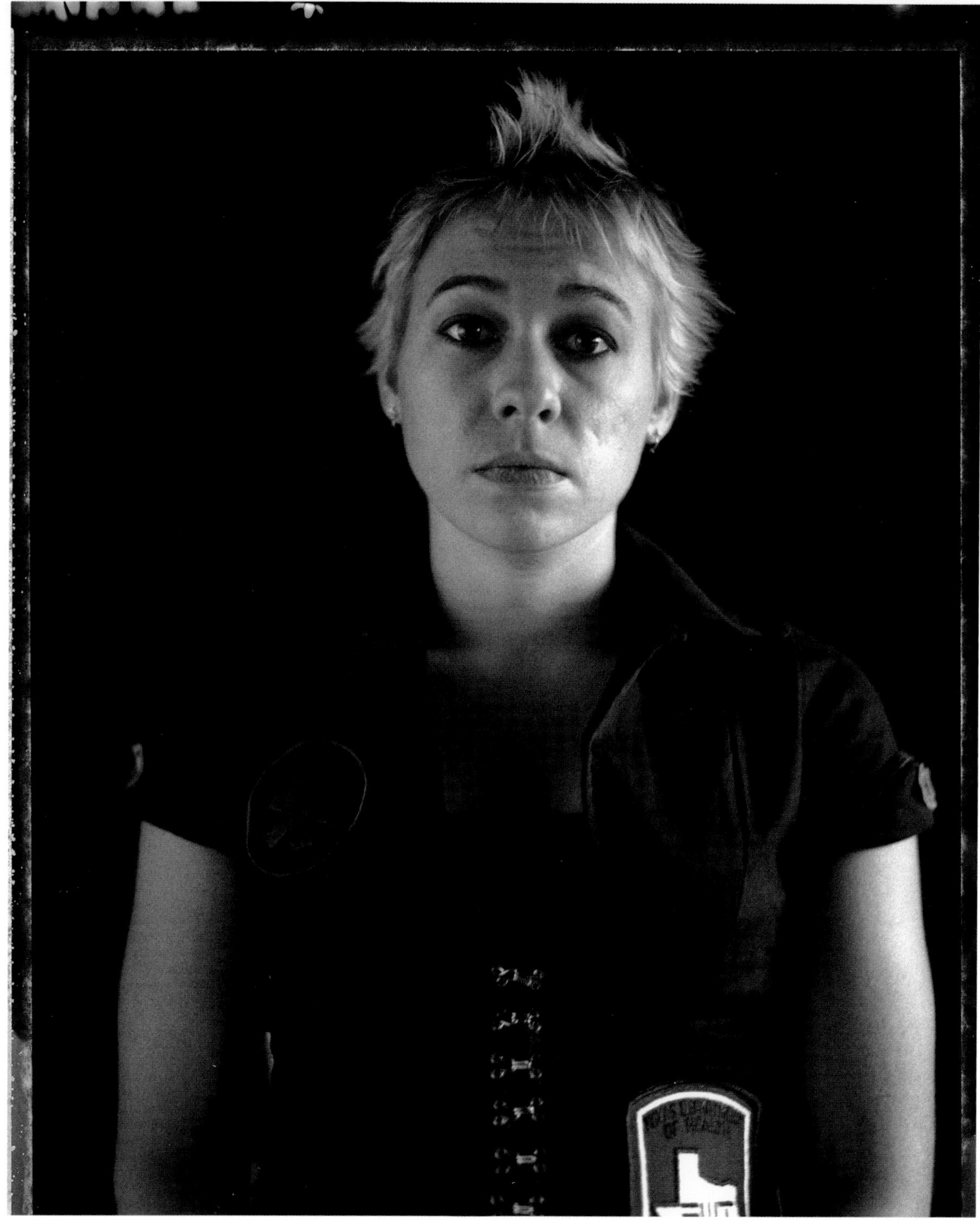

Carmen Geddit

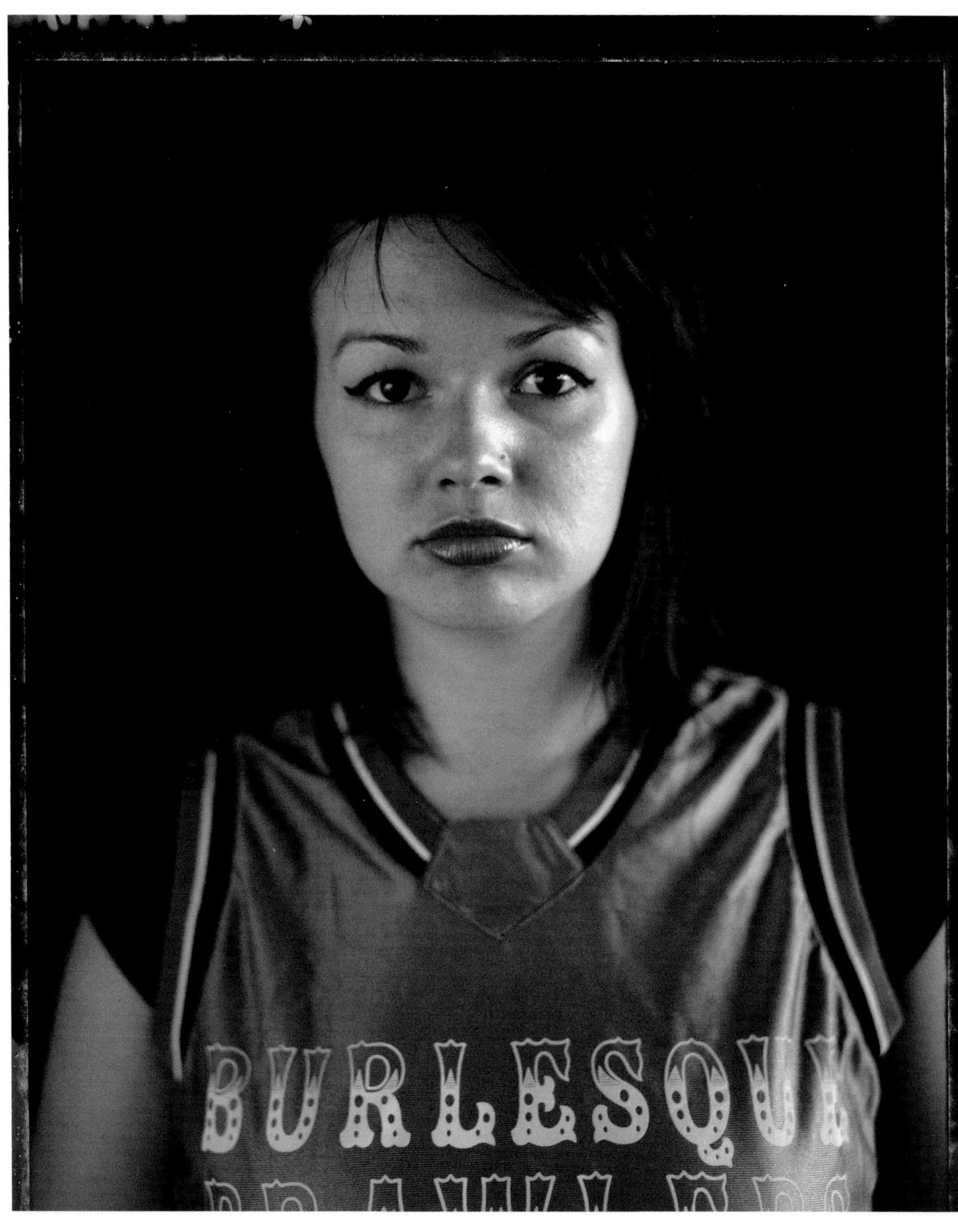

disMae West

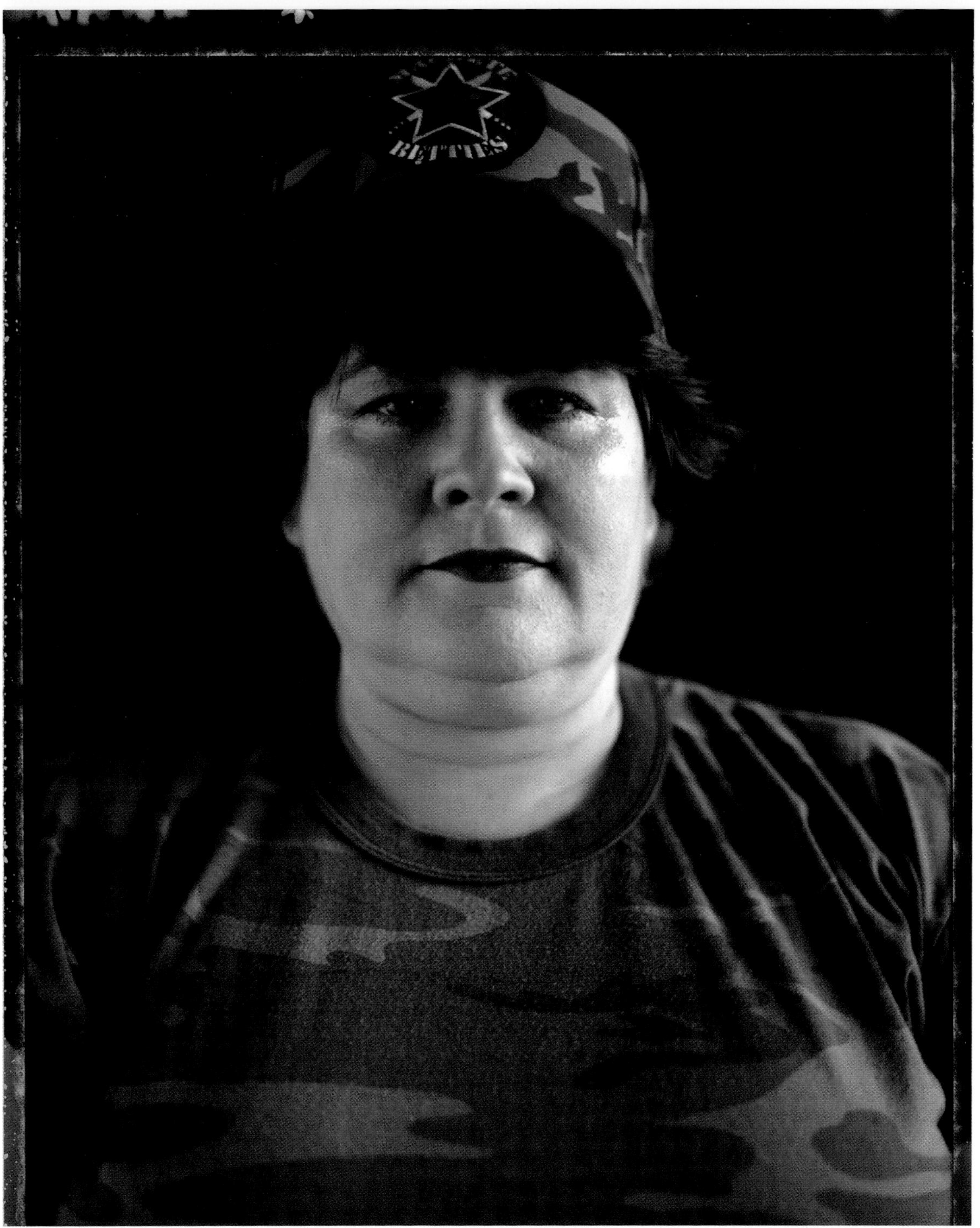

Madam M

"There are guys around the rink that just want to marry a Derby Girl."

"Take your calcium; you need strong bones to be a Derby Girl."

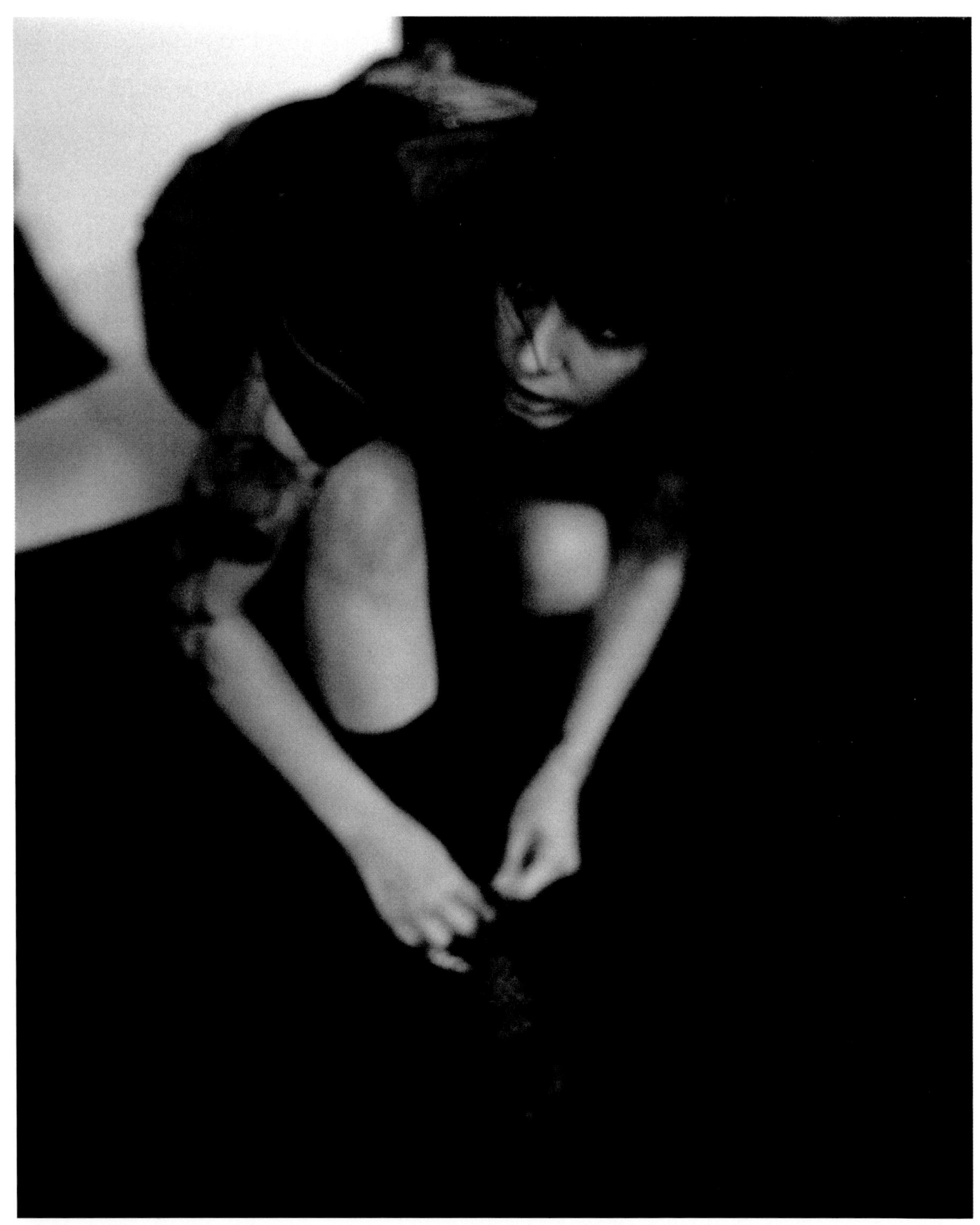

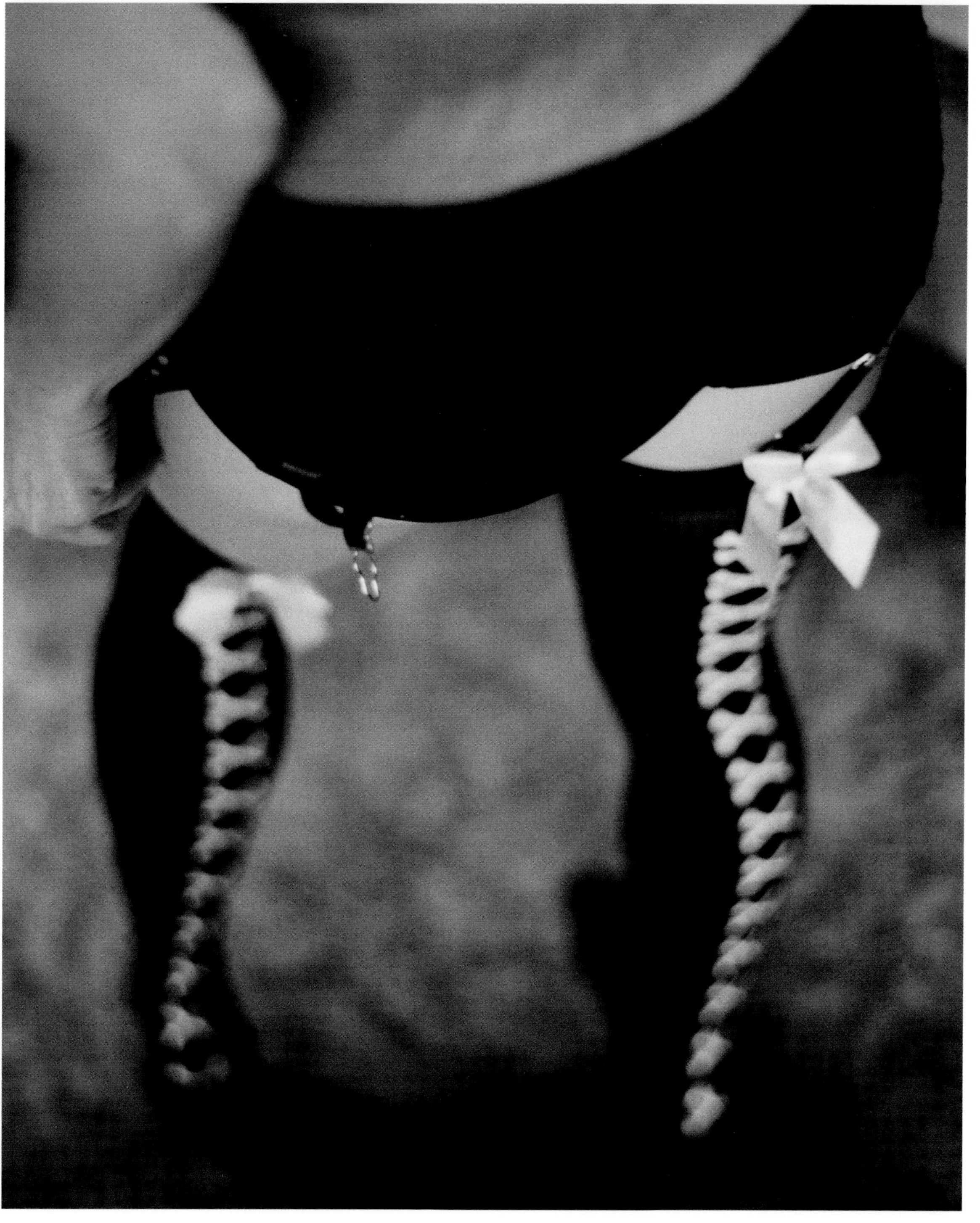

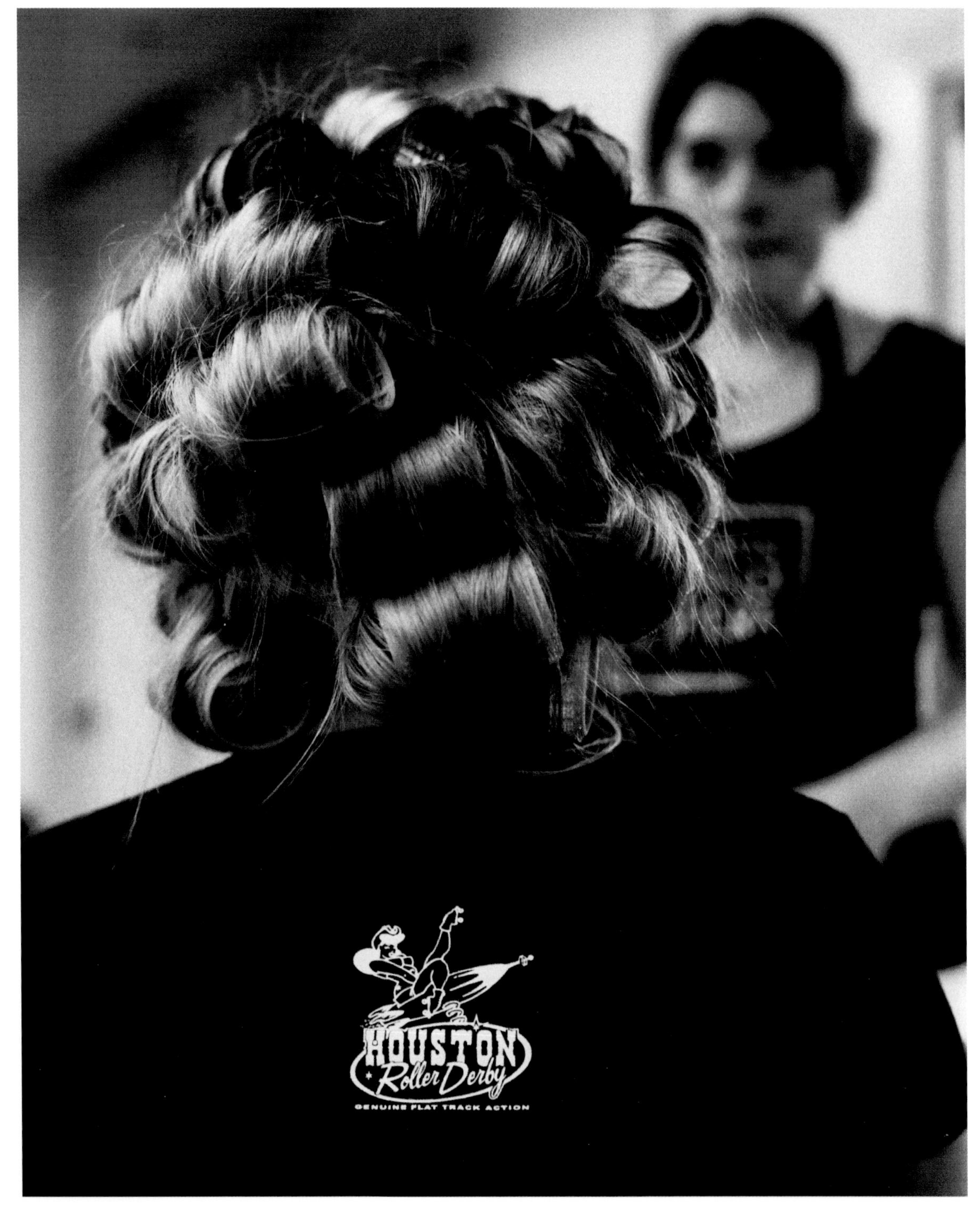

HOUSTON
Roller Derby
GENUINE FLAT TRACK ACTION

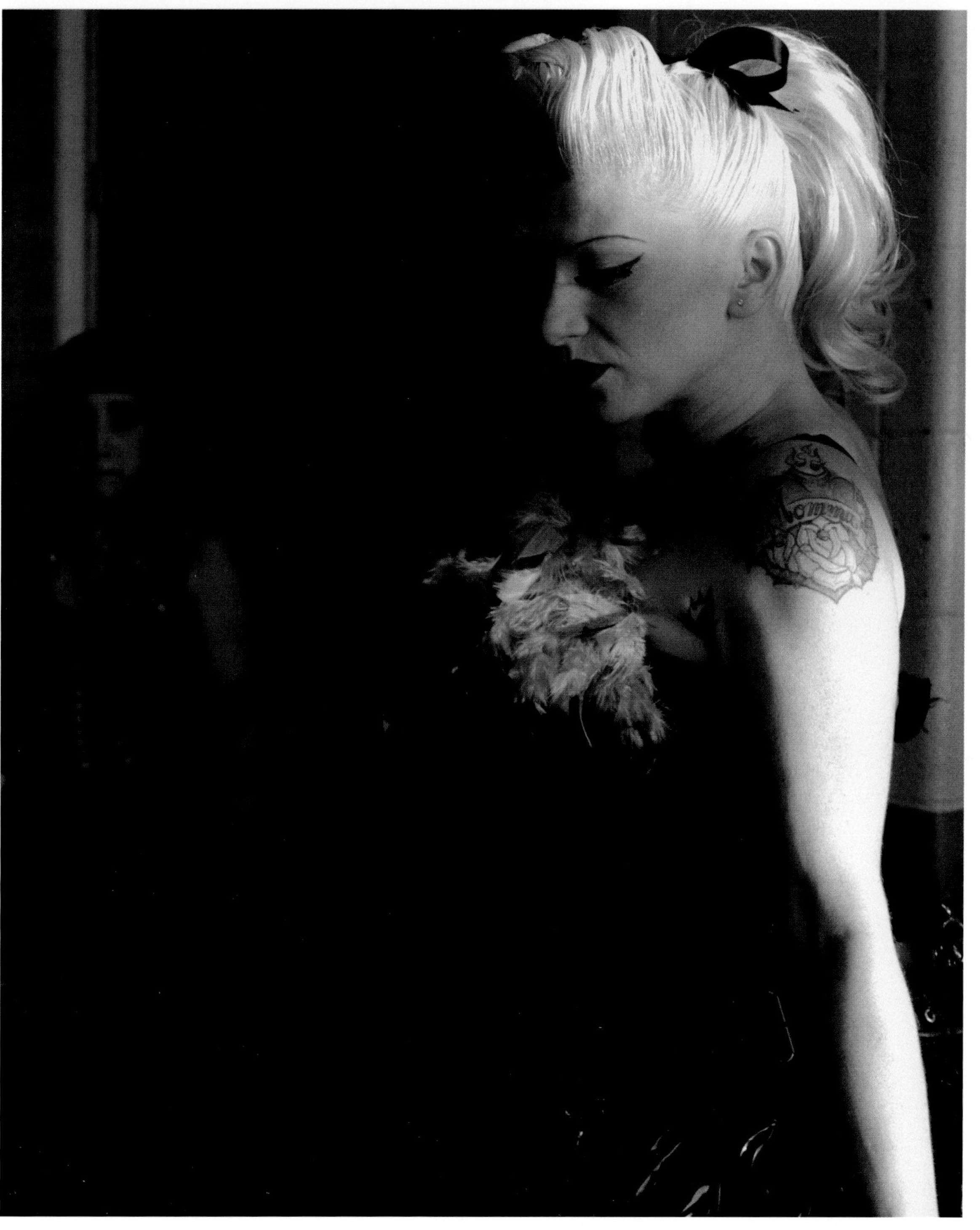

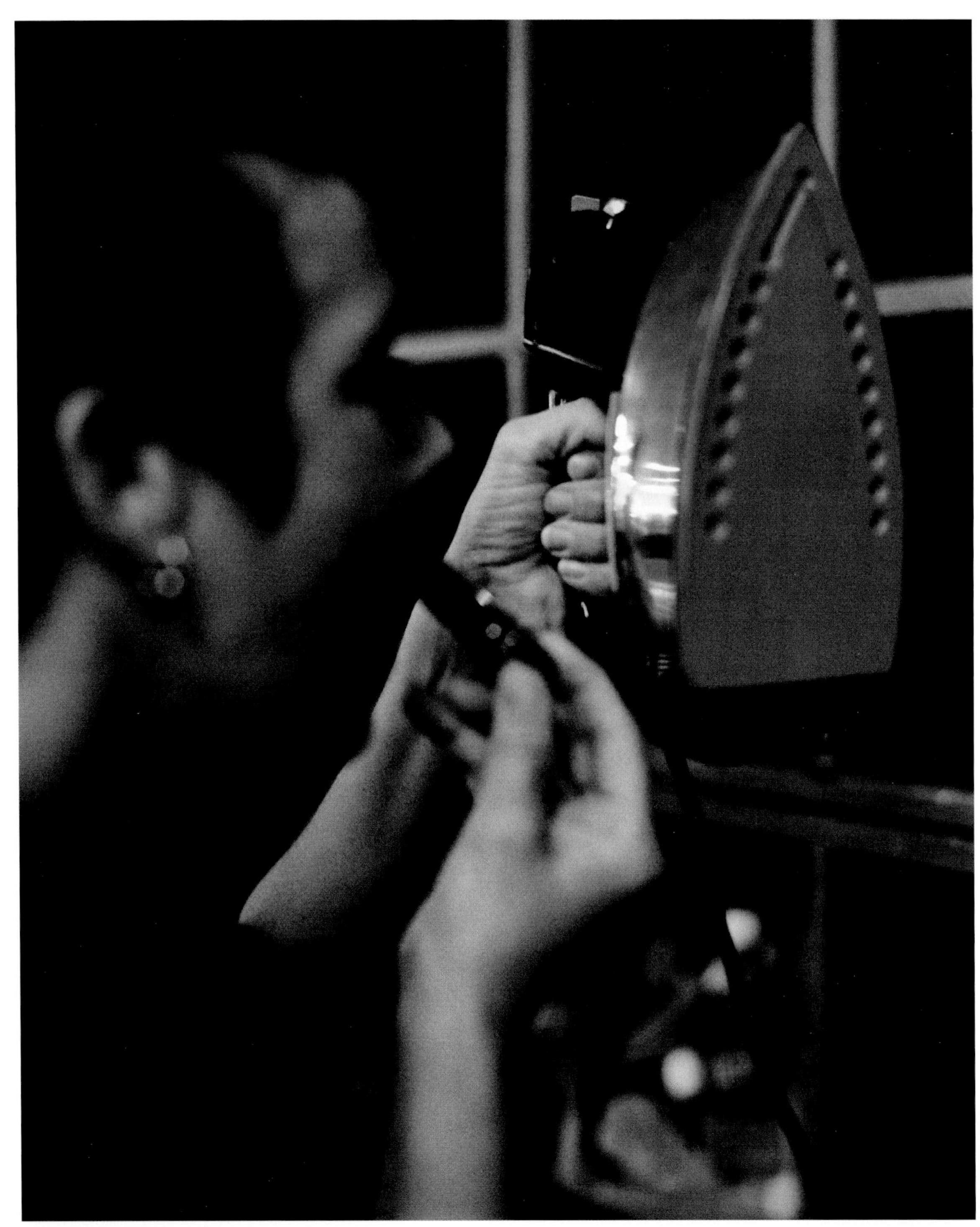

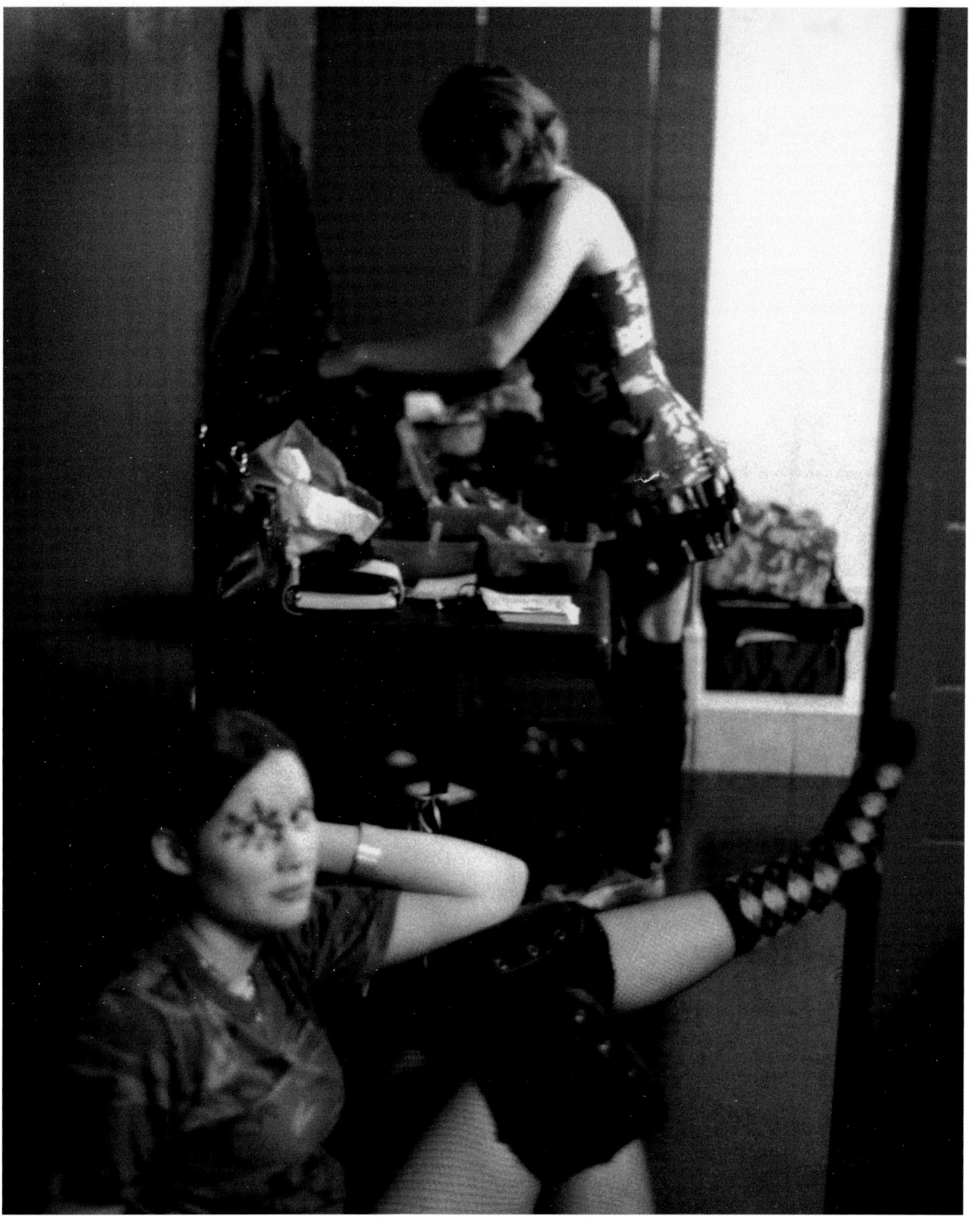

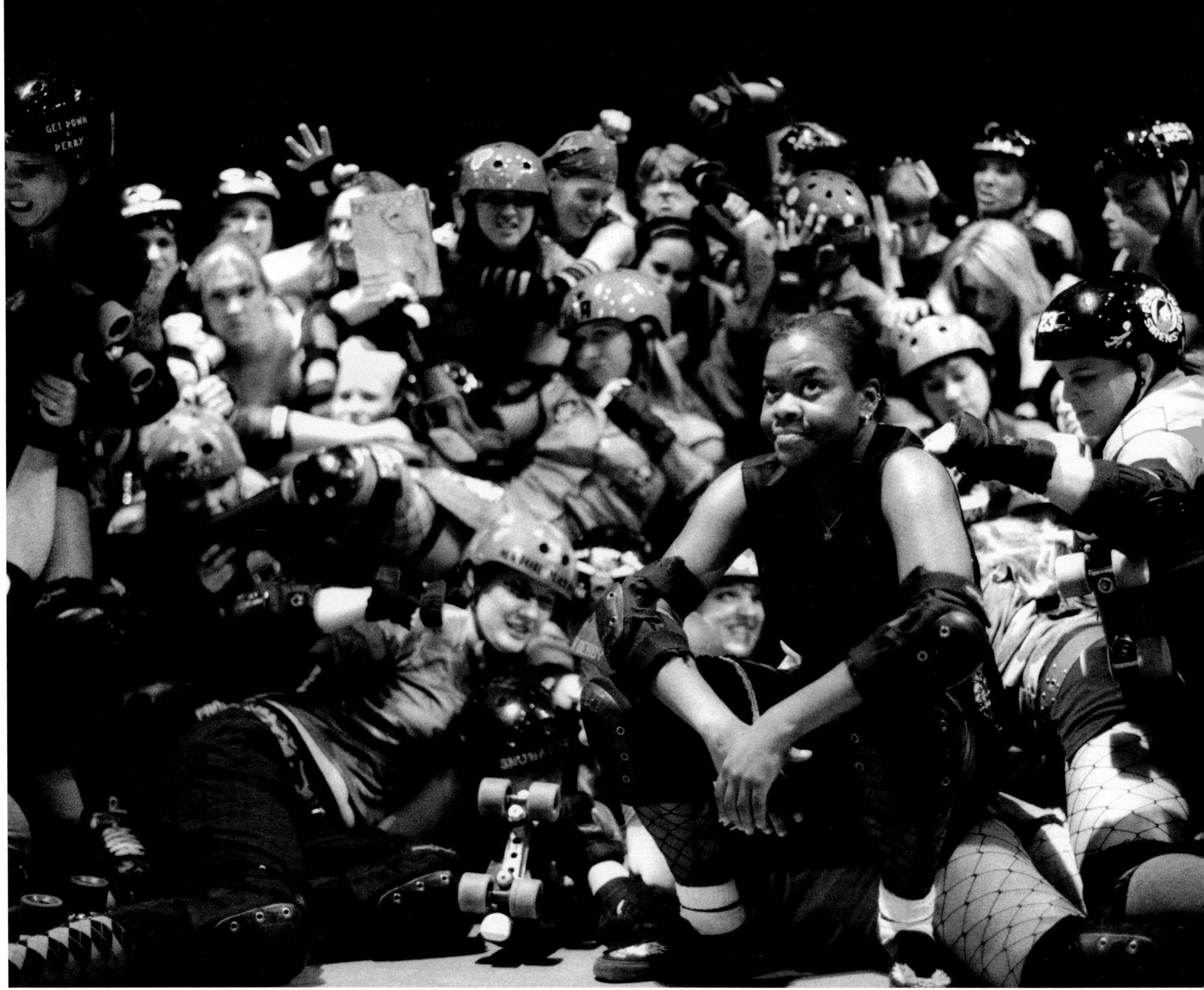

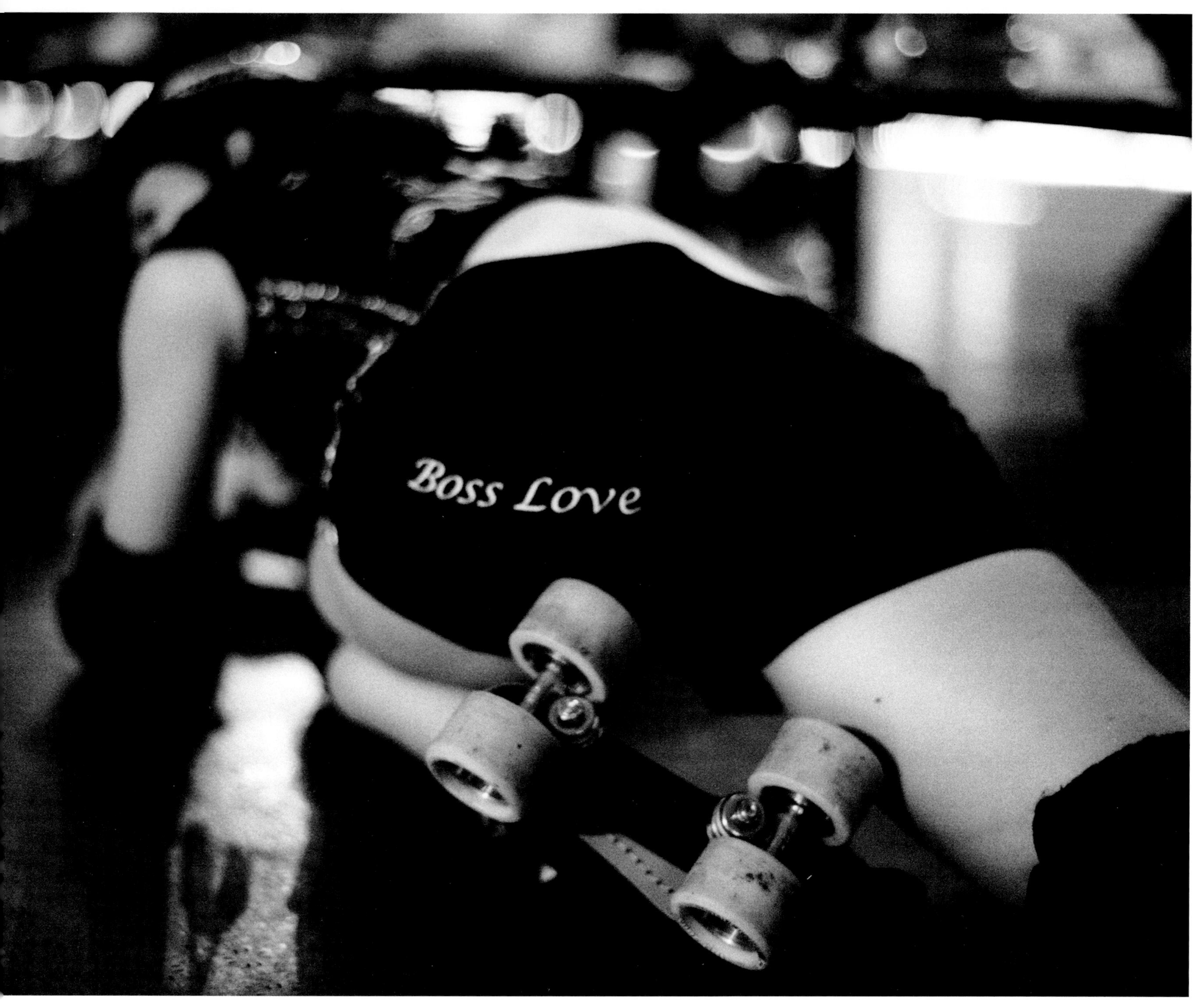
Boss Love

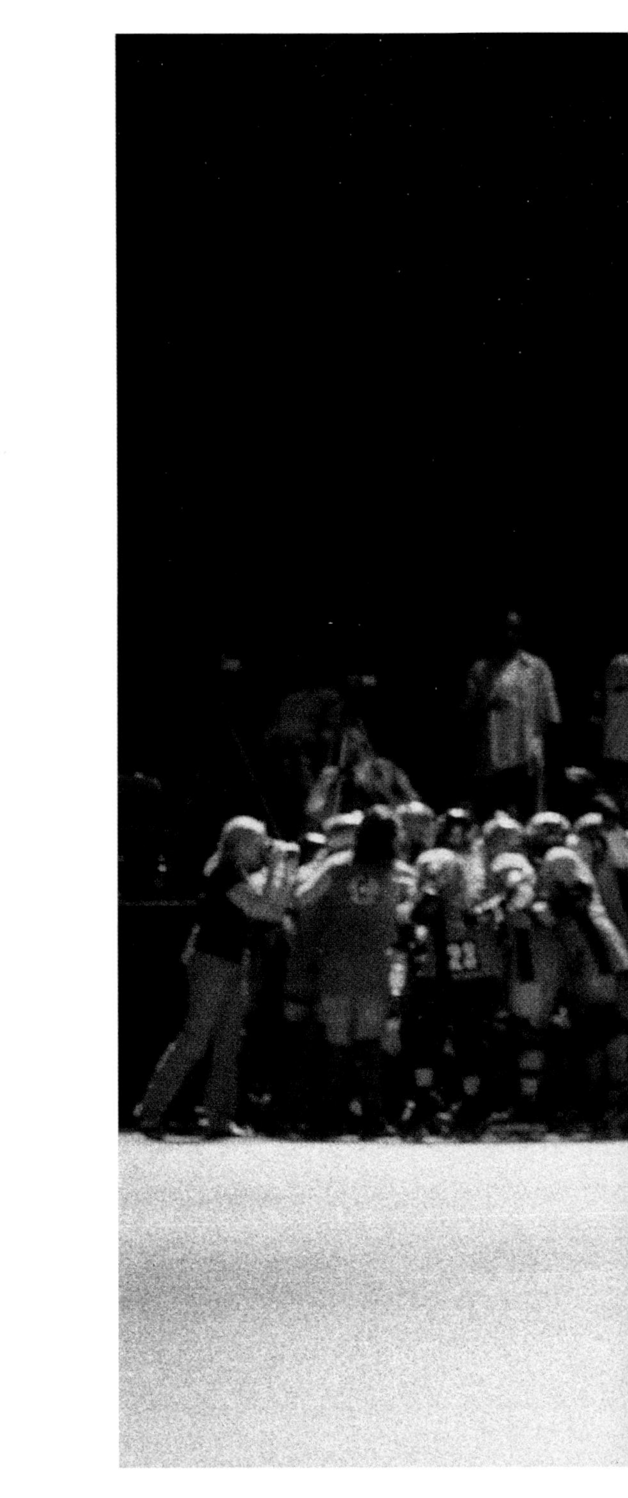

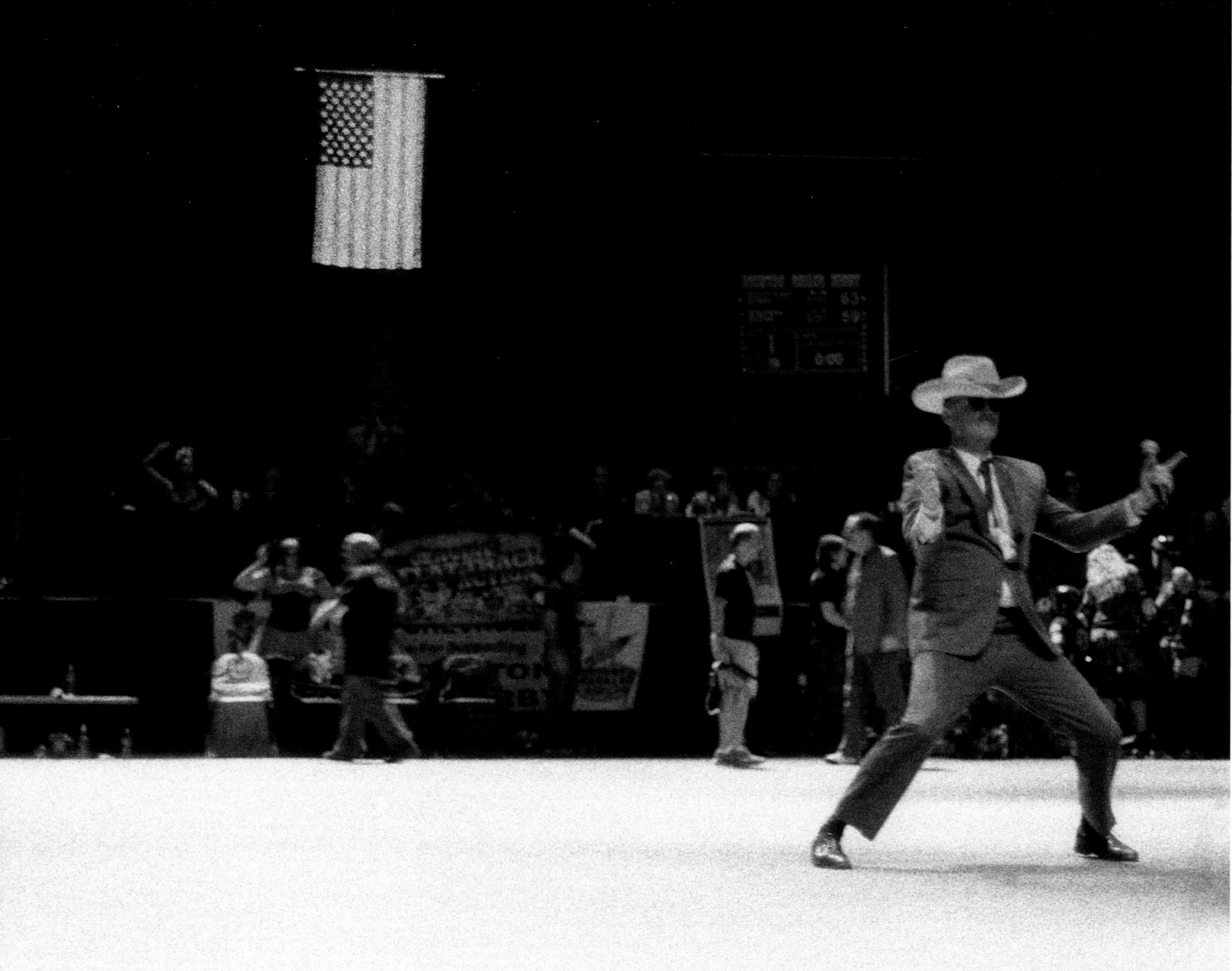

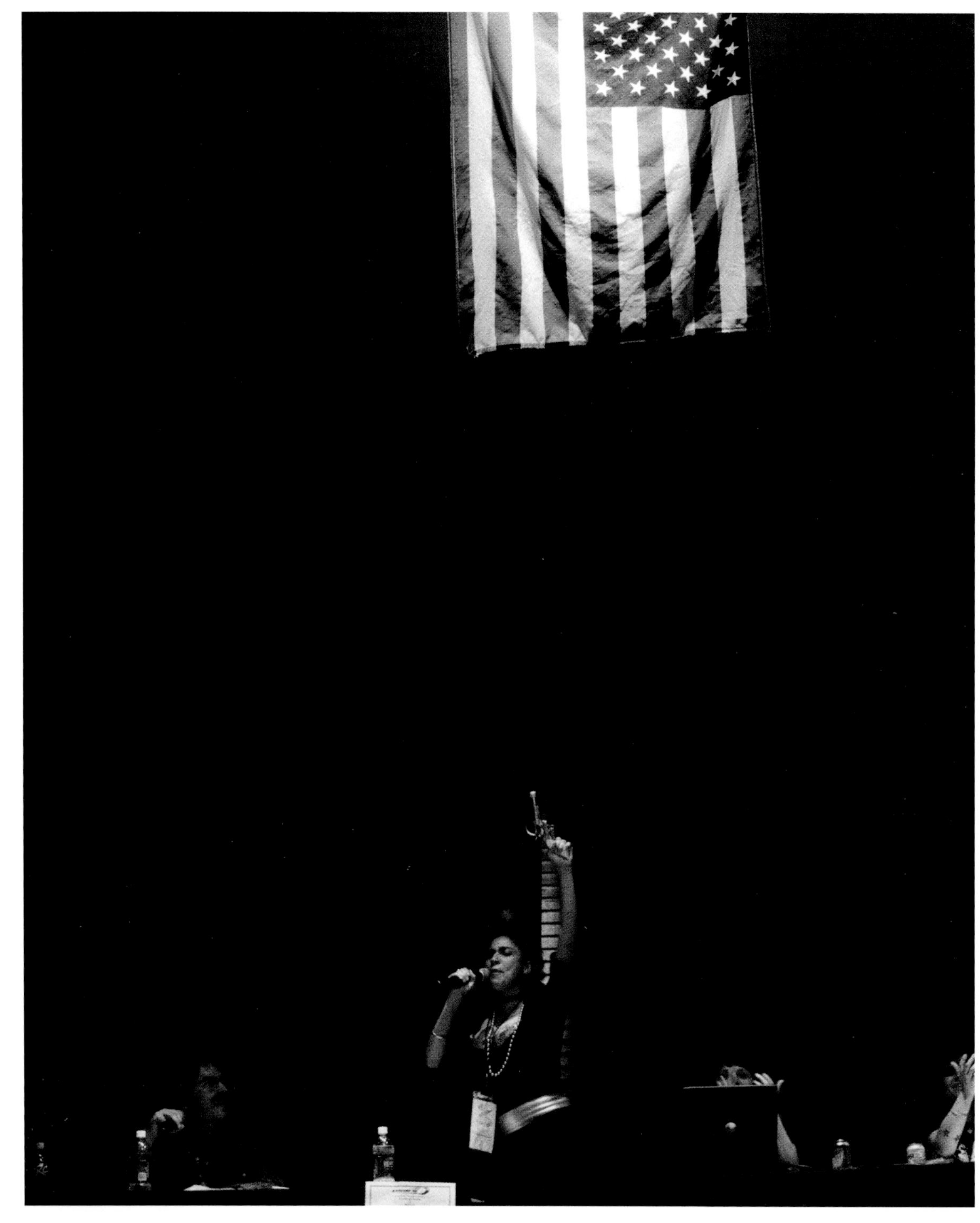

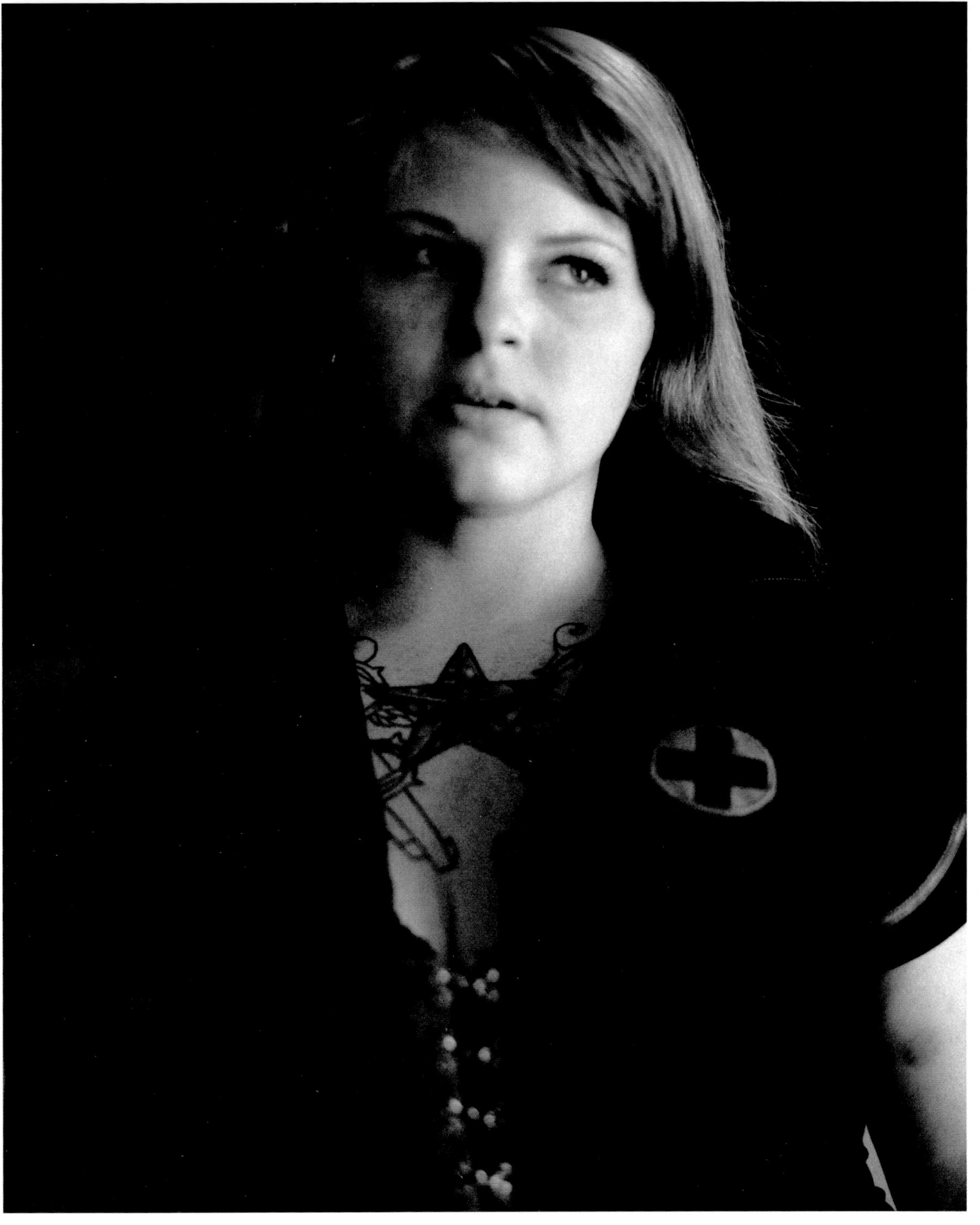

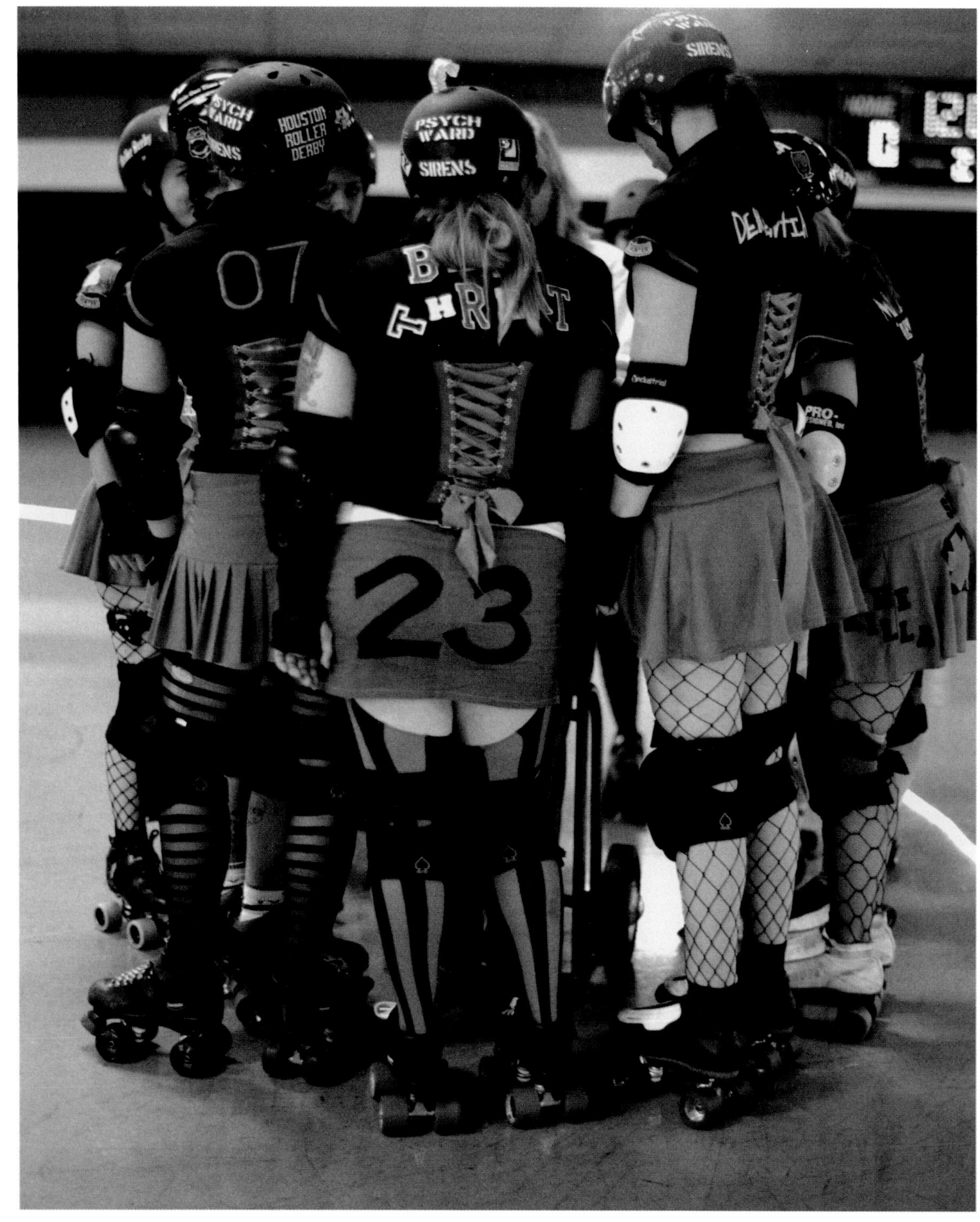

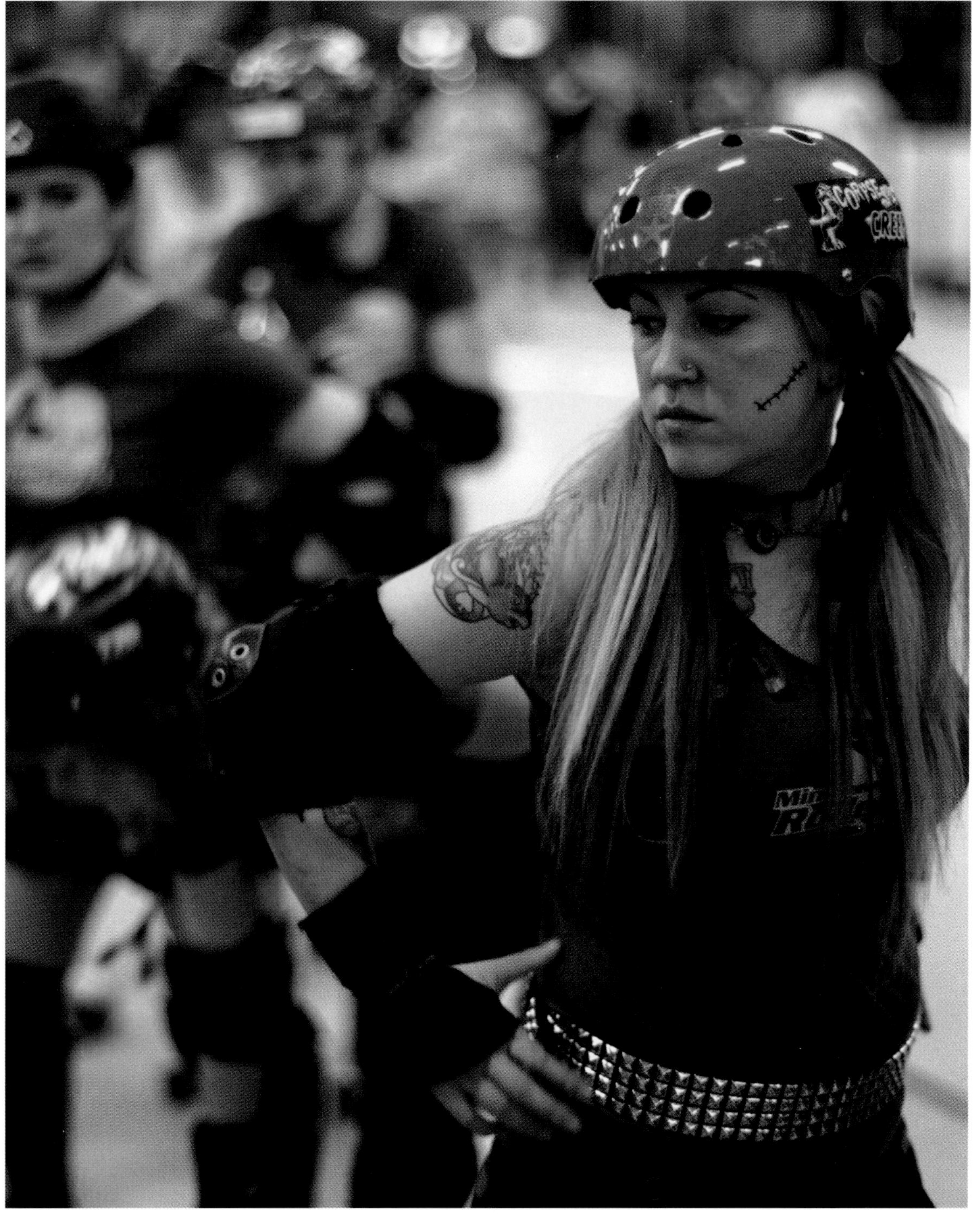

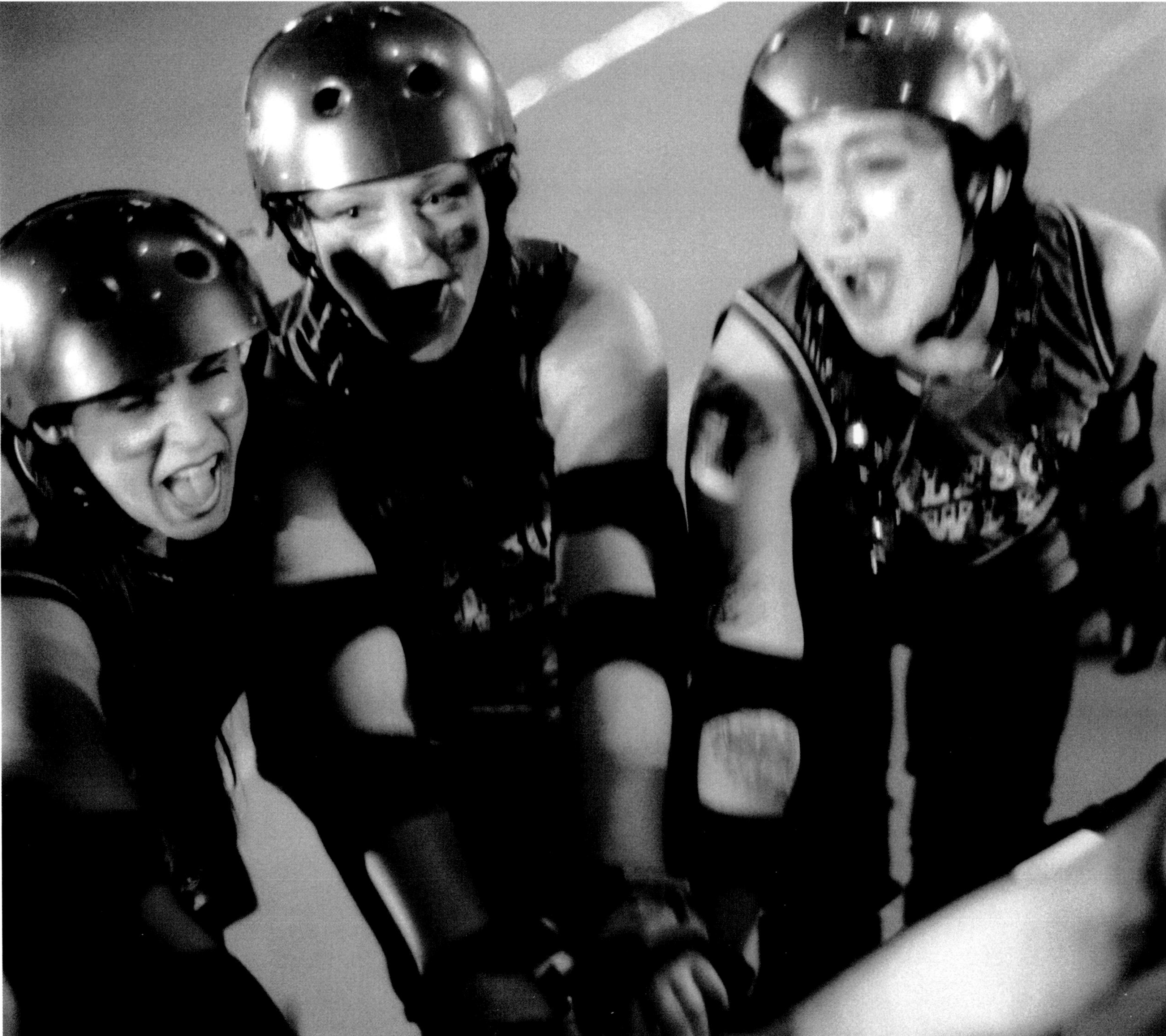

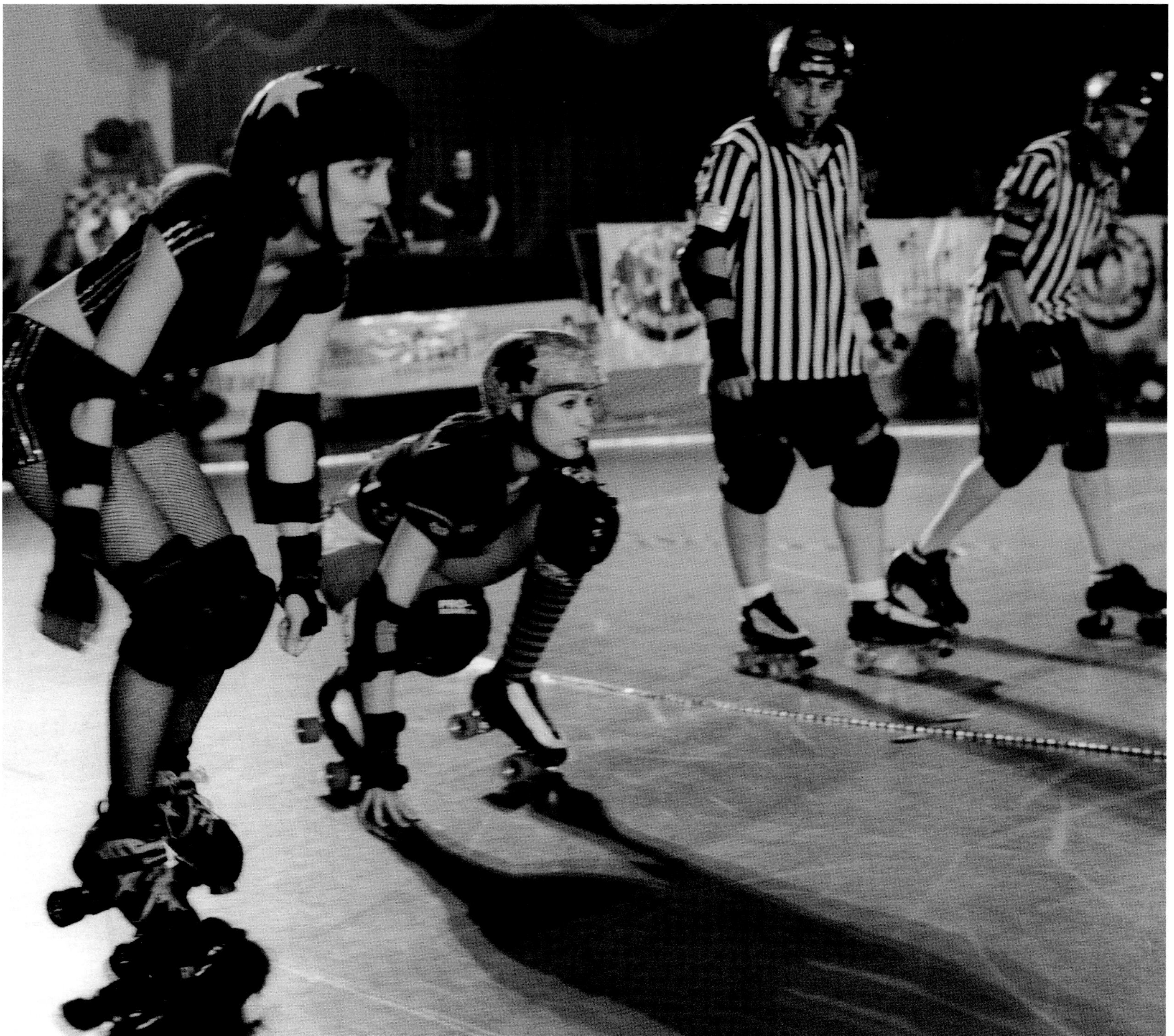

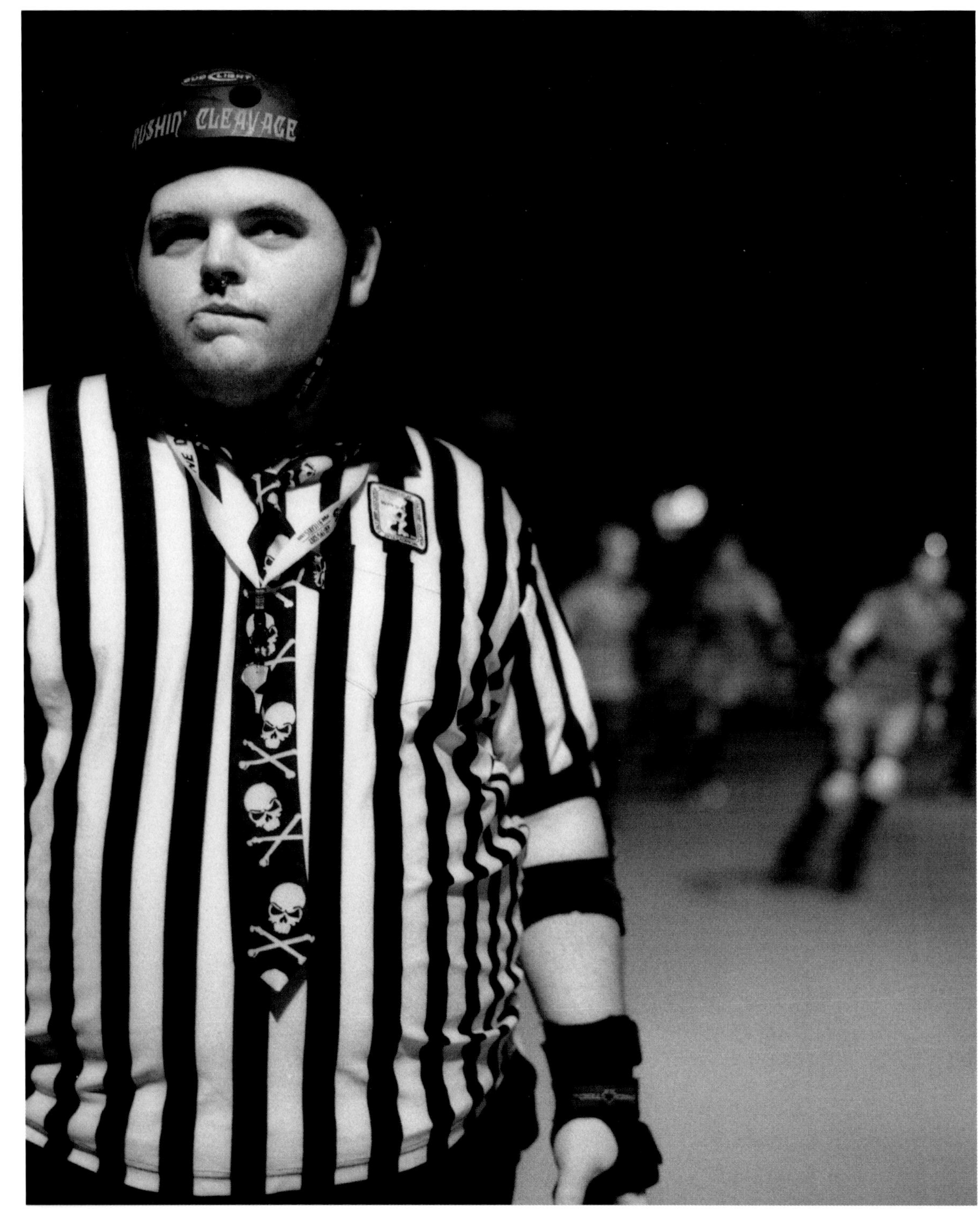
RUSHIN' CLEAVAGE

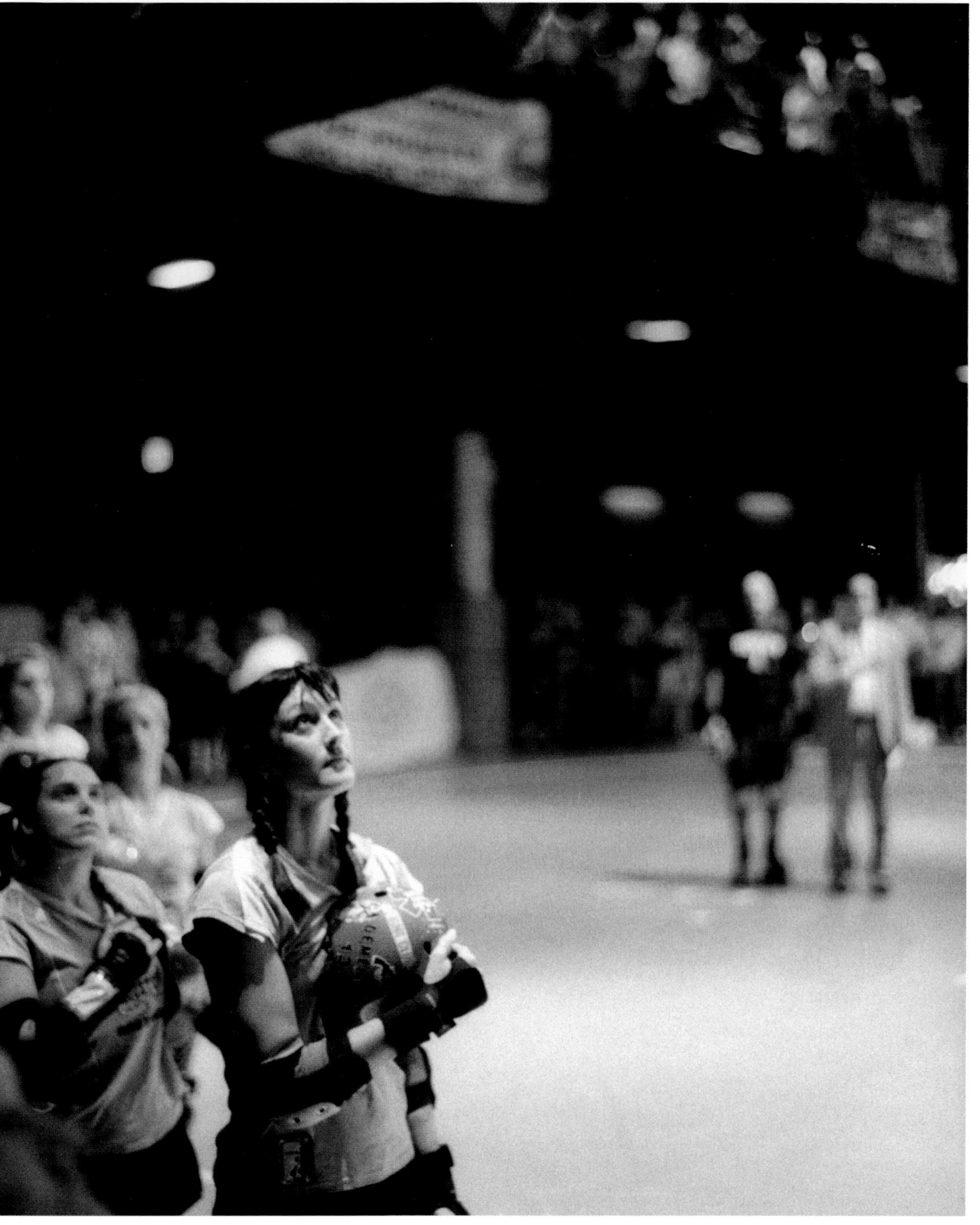

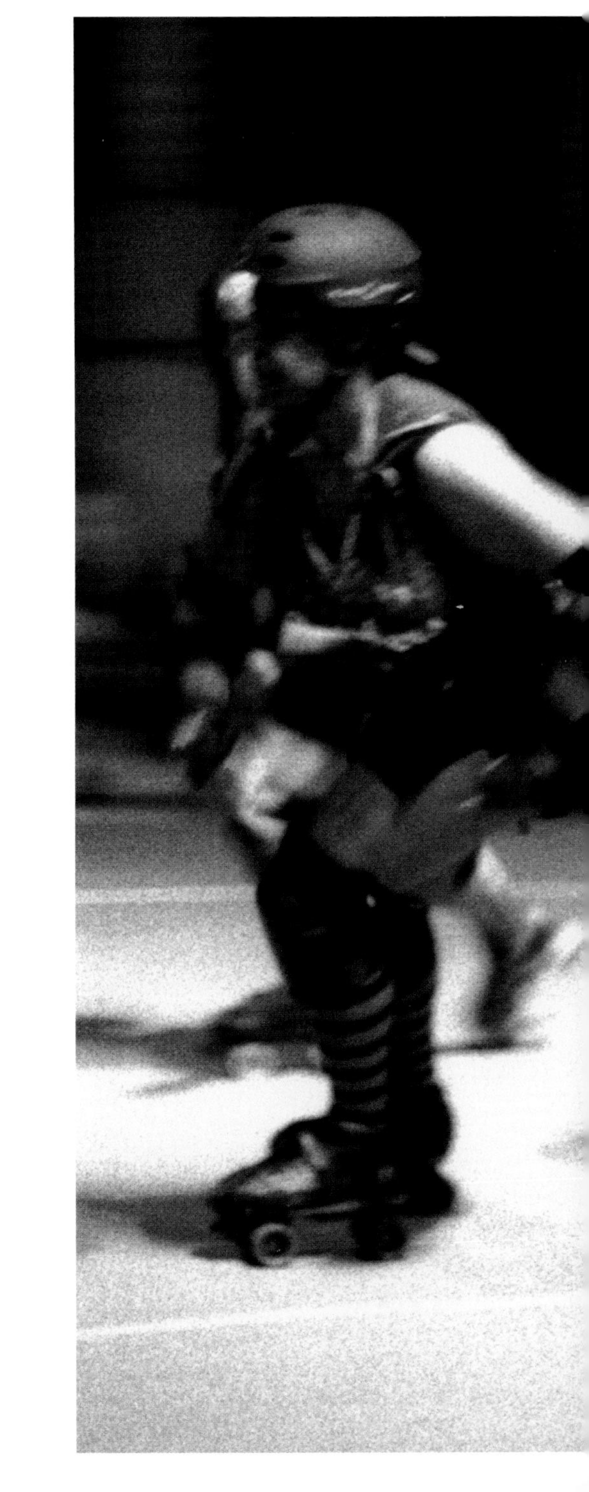

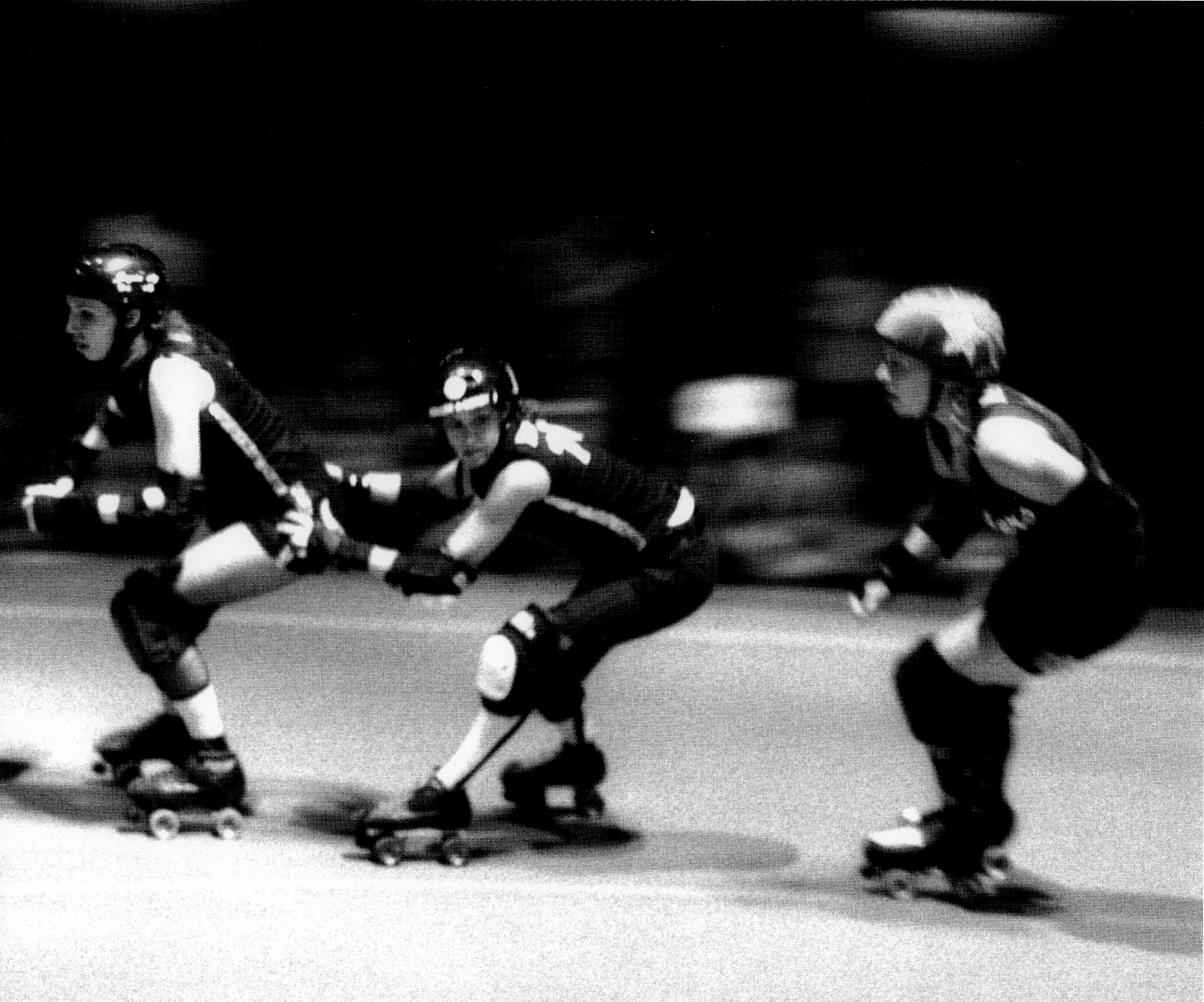

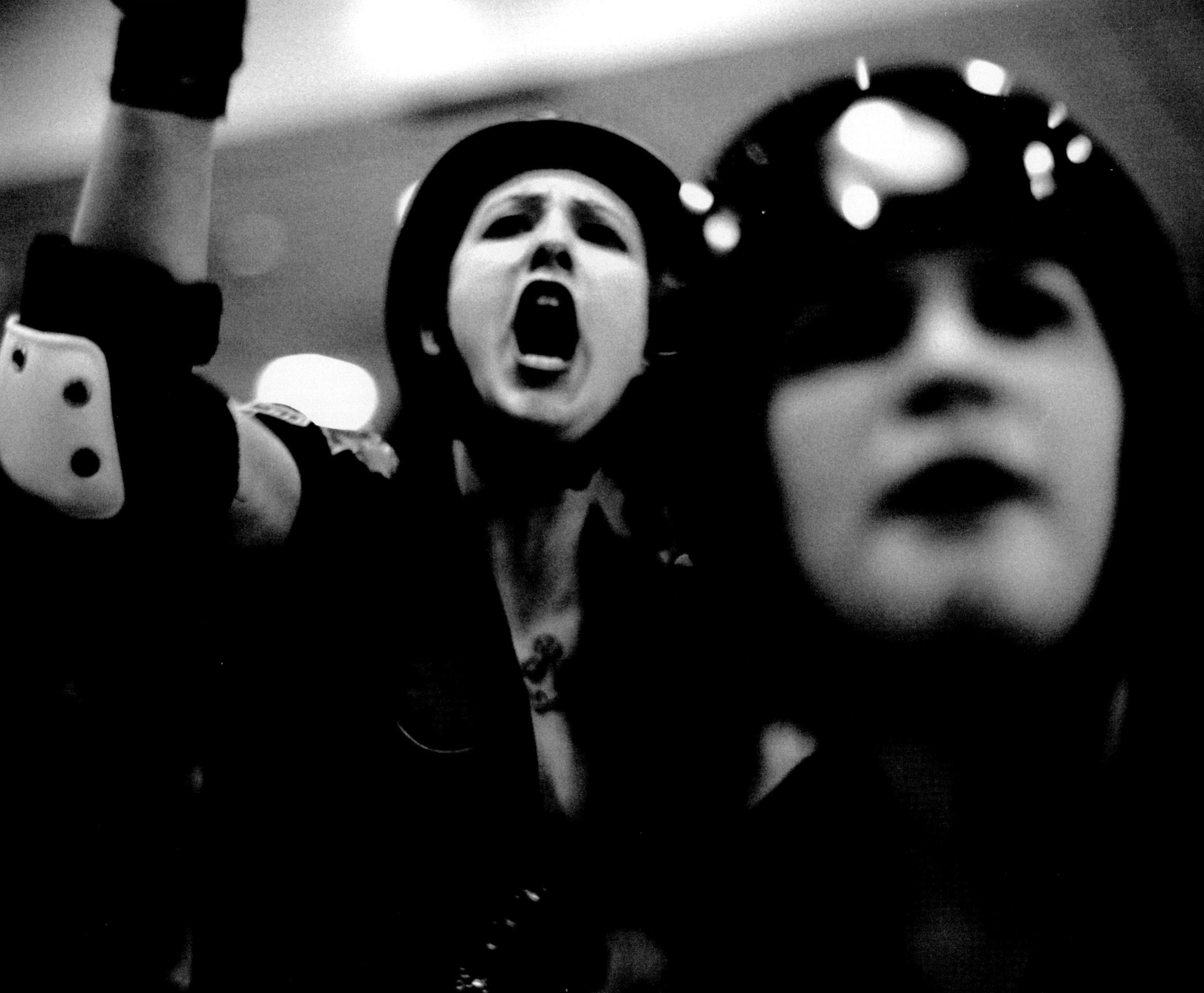

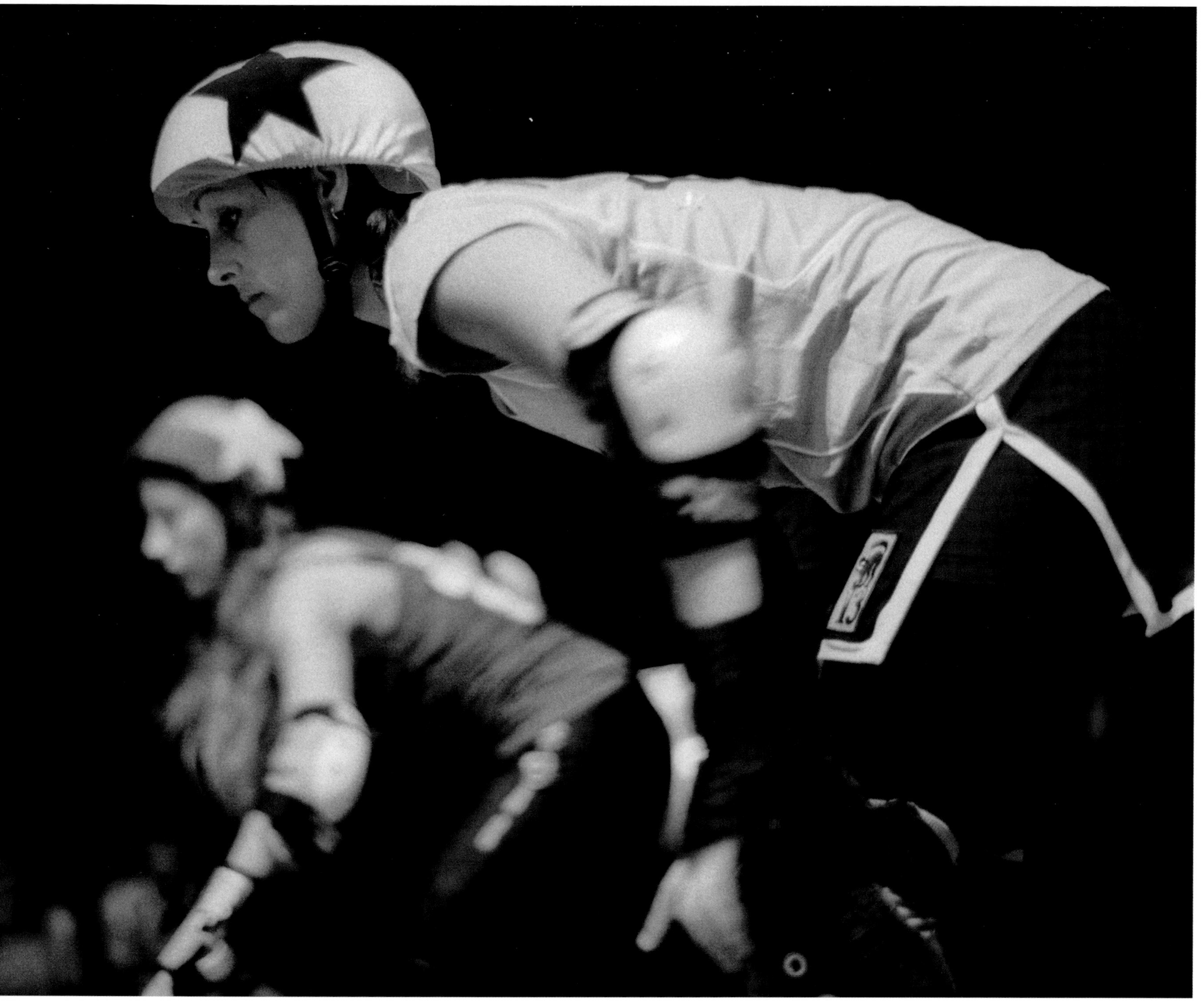

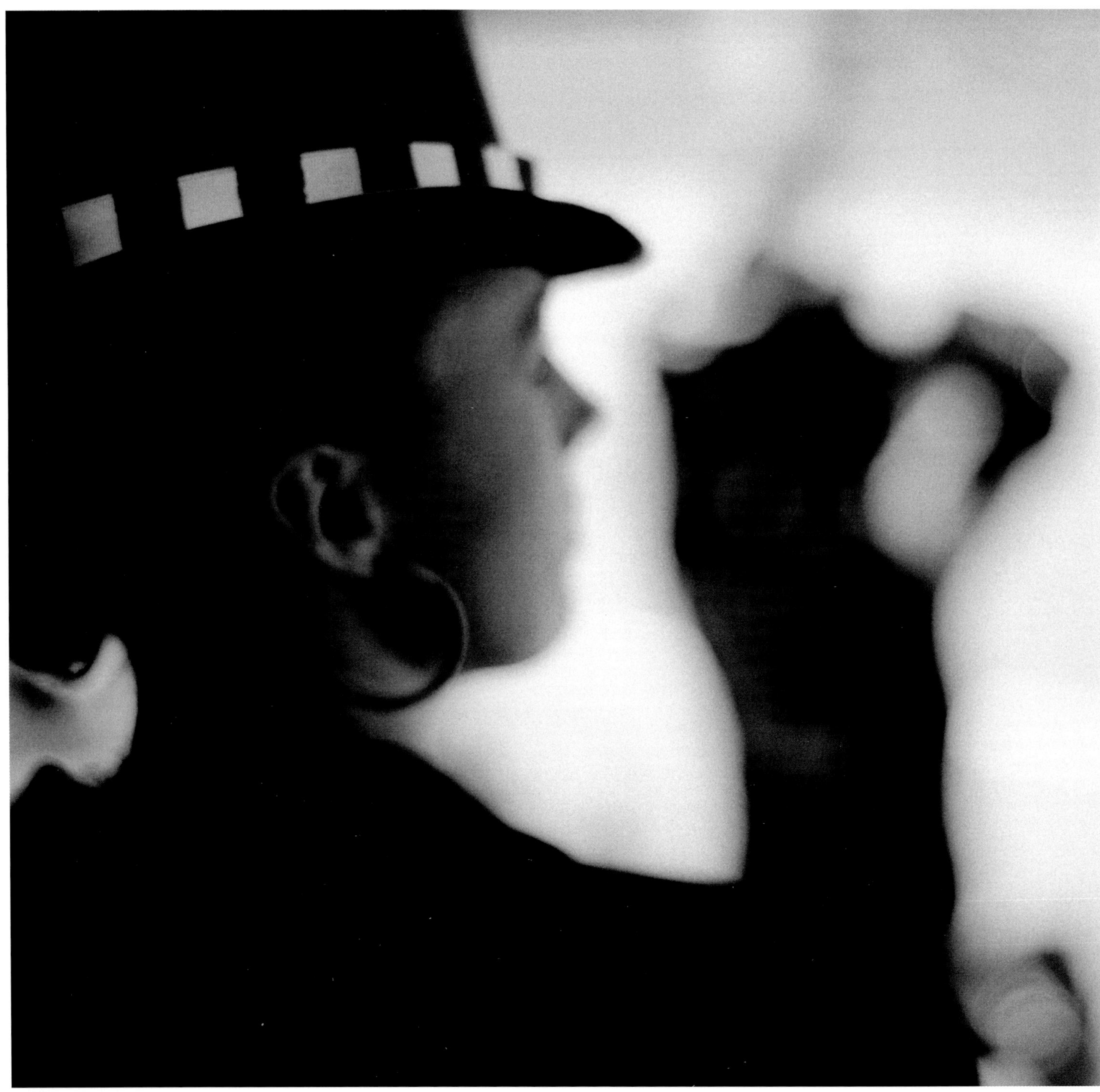

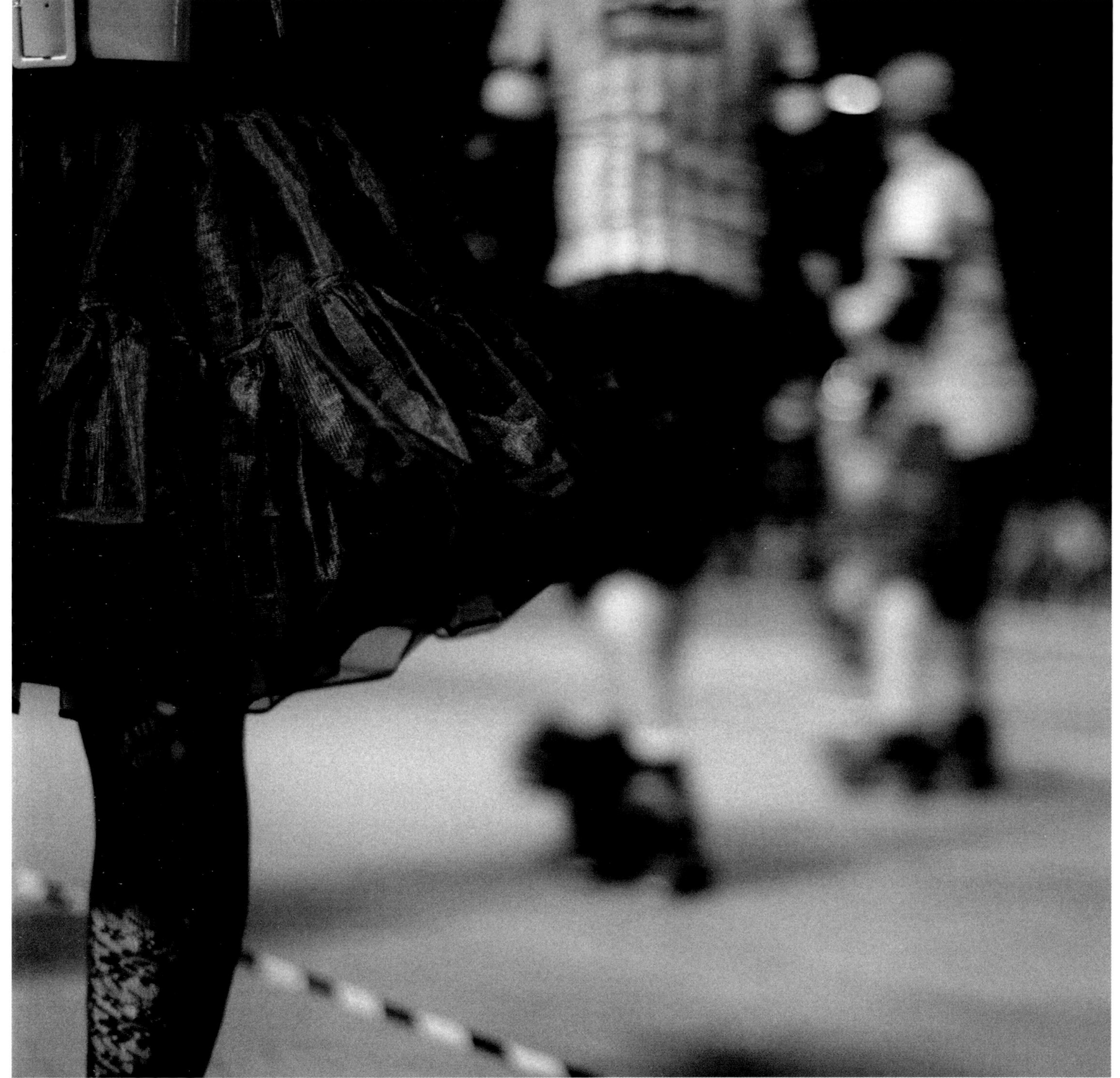

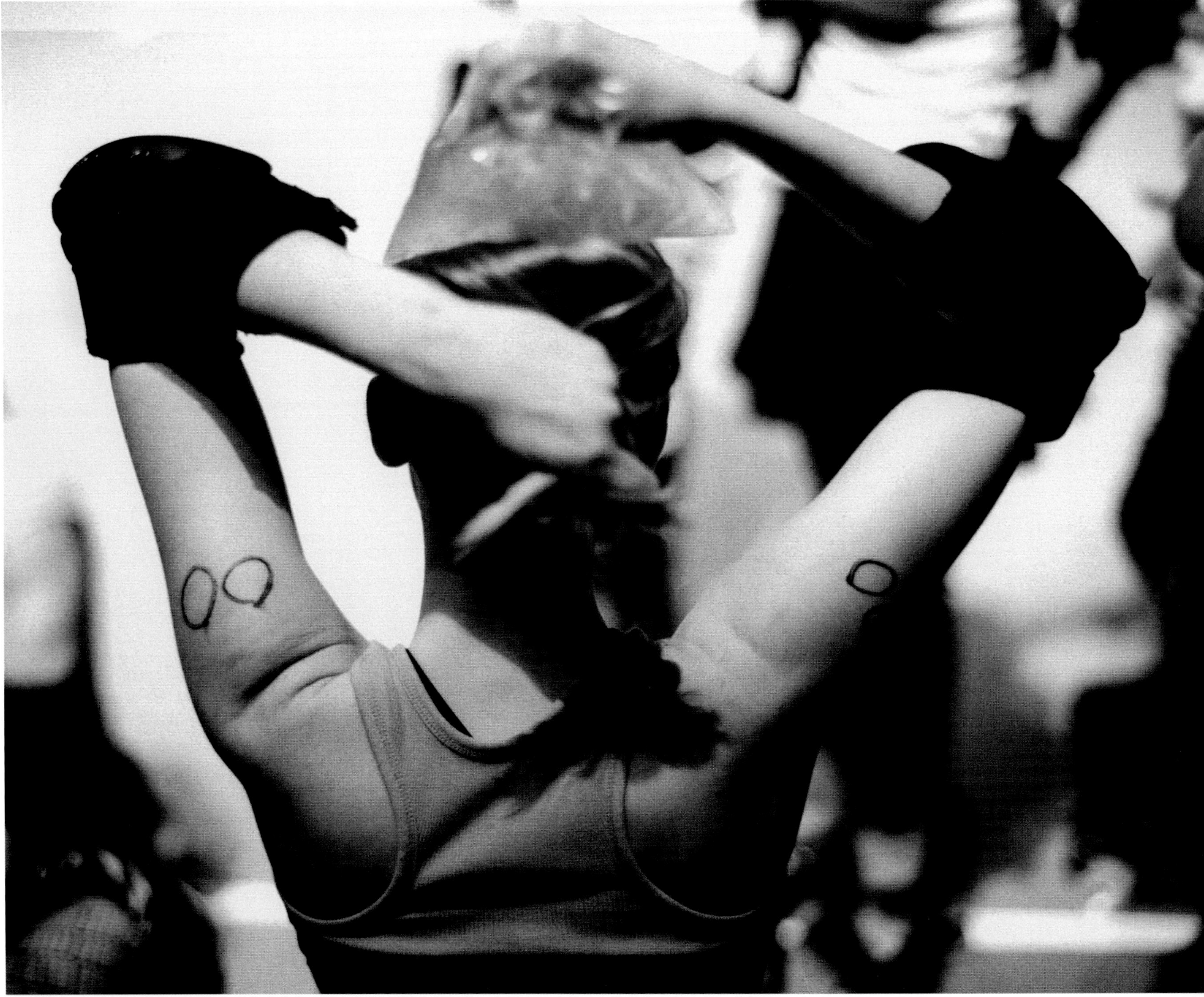

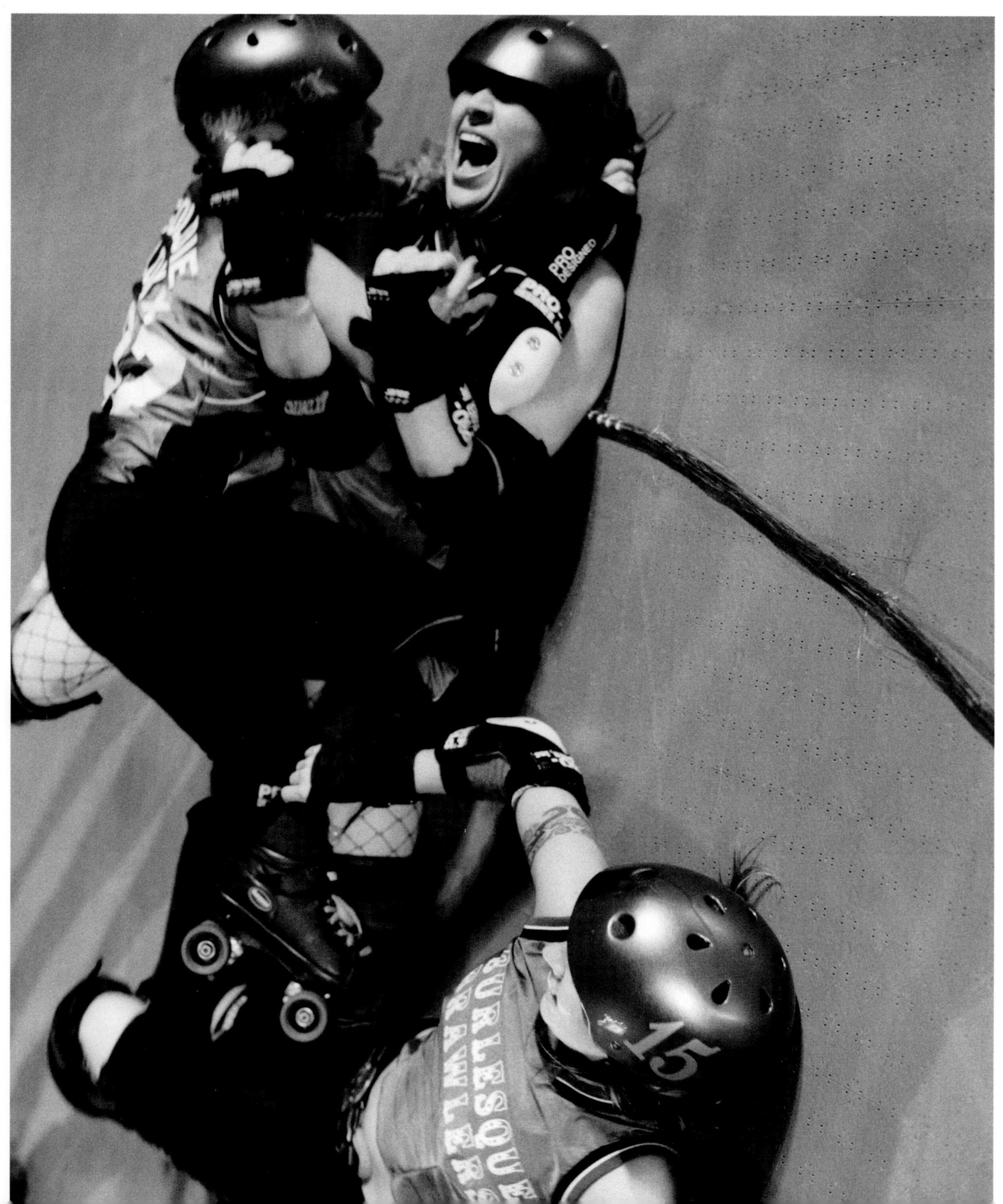

PRO DESIGNED
BURLESQUE BRAWLERS
15

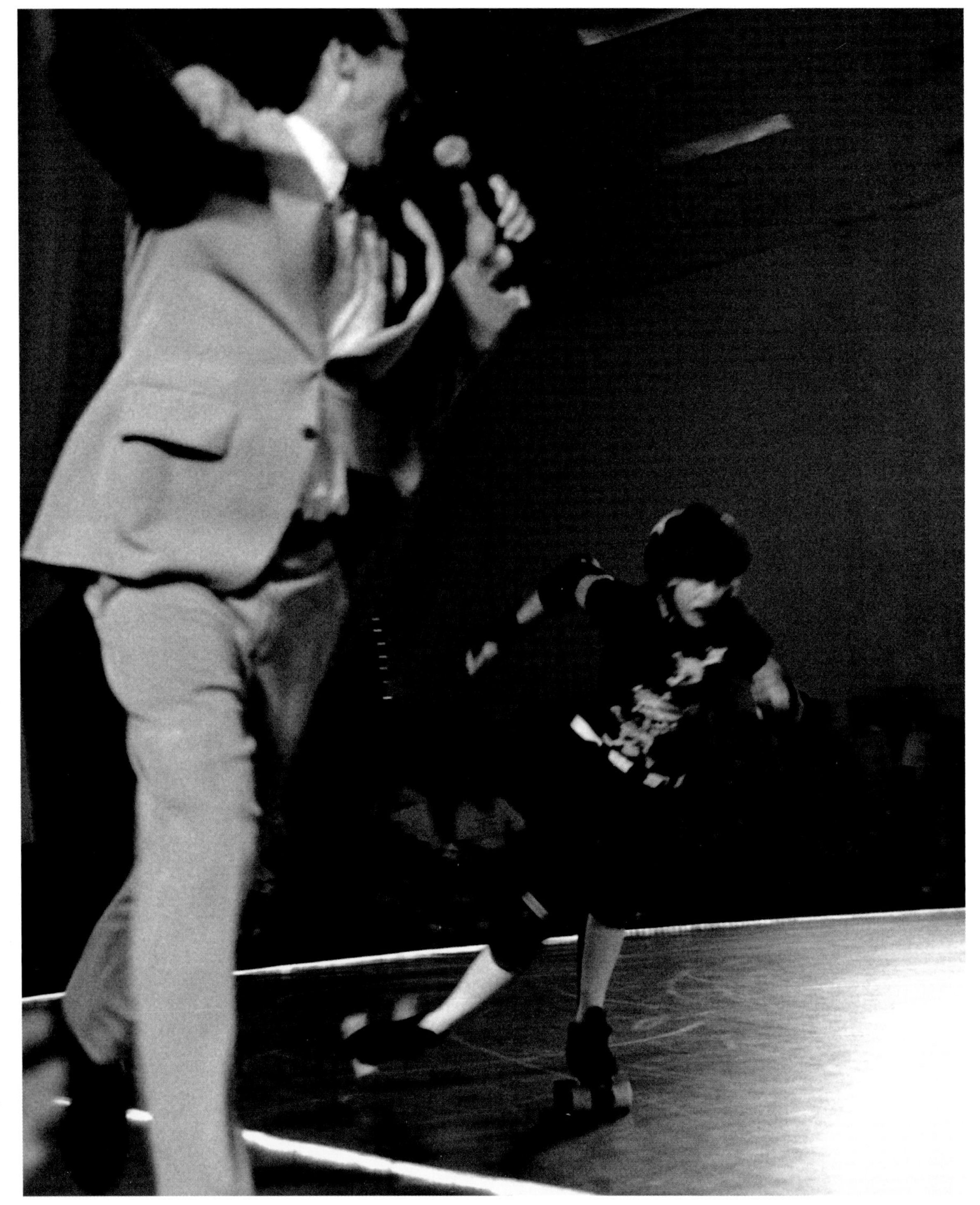

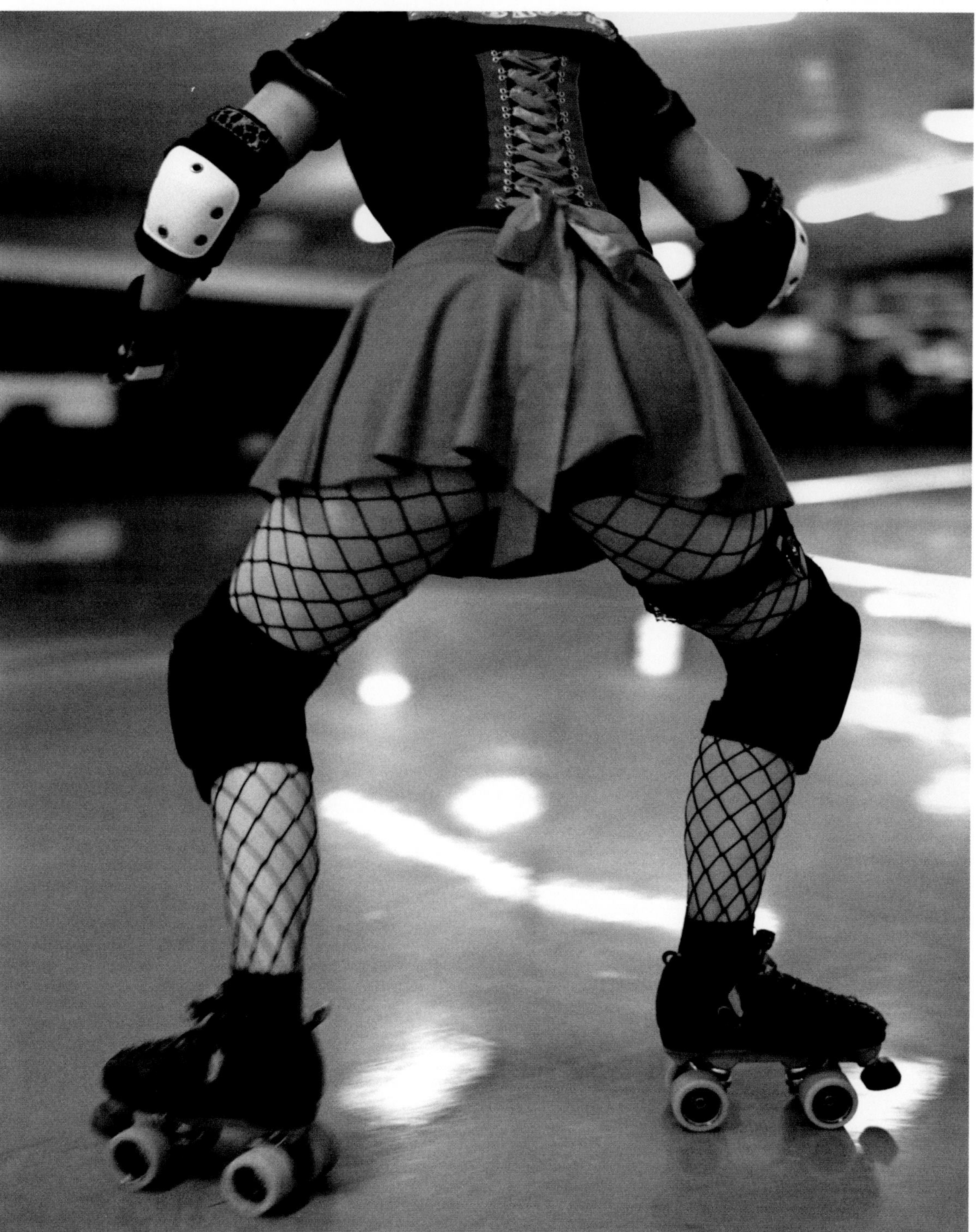

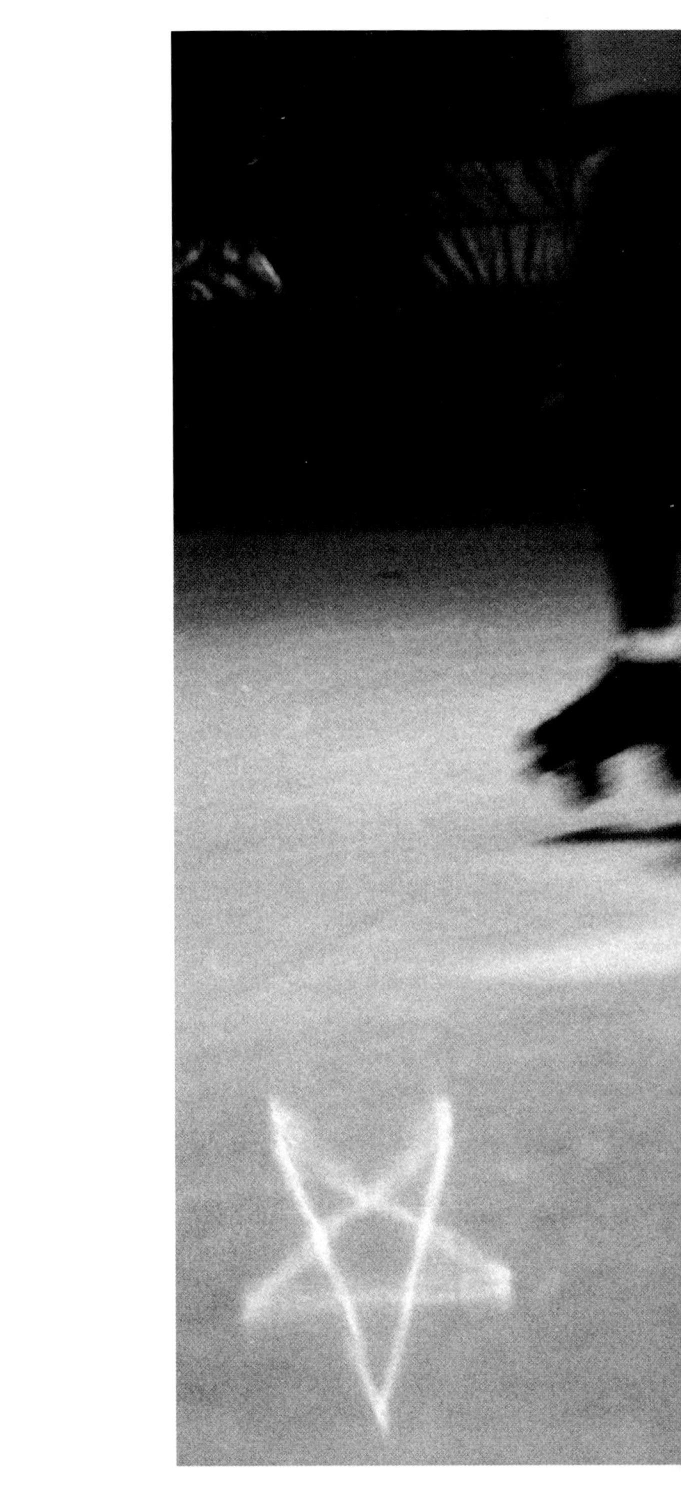

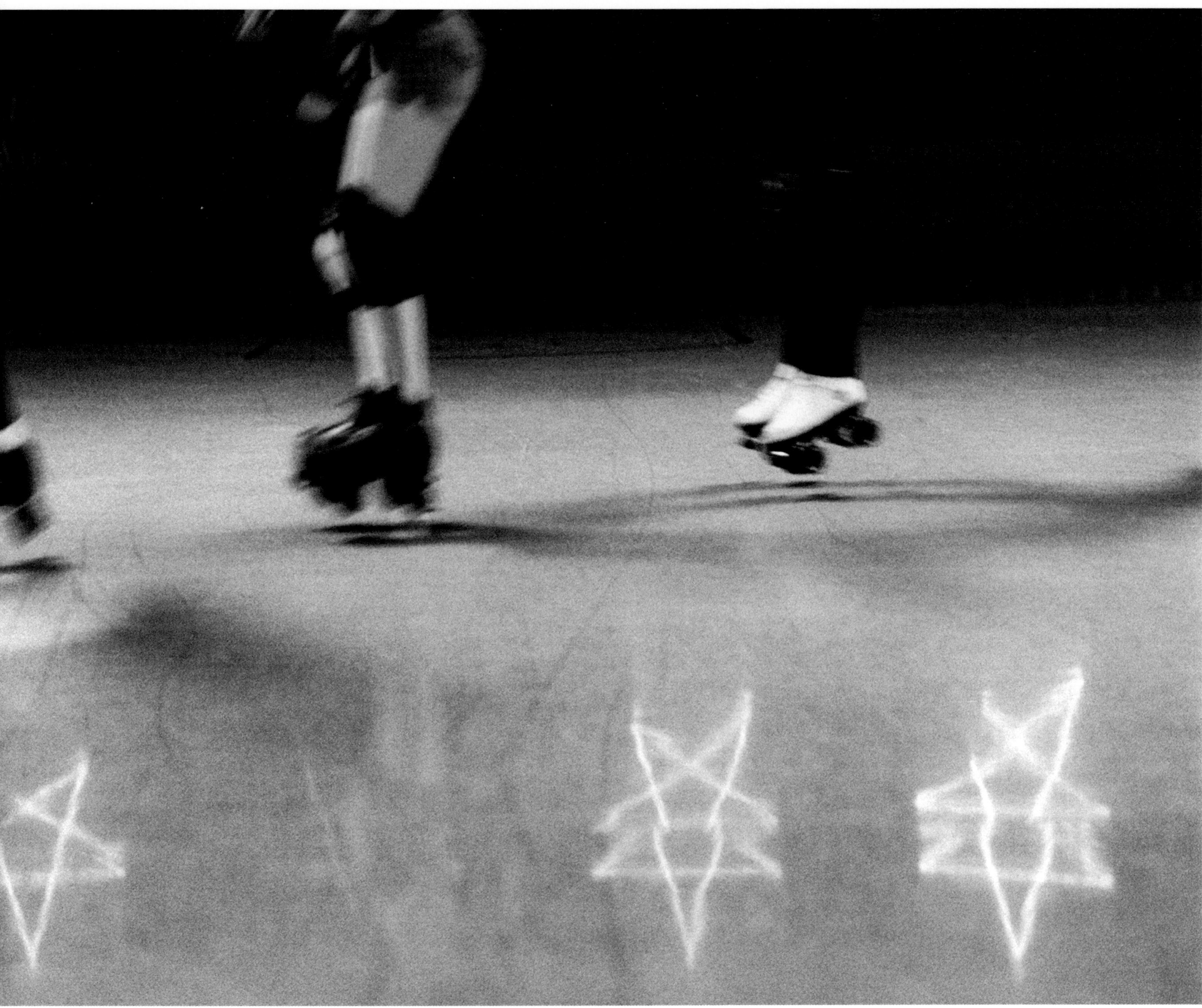

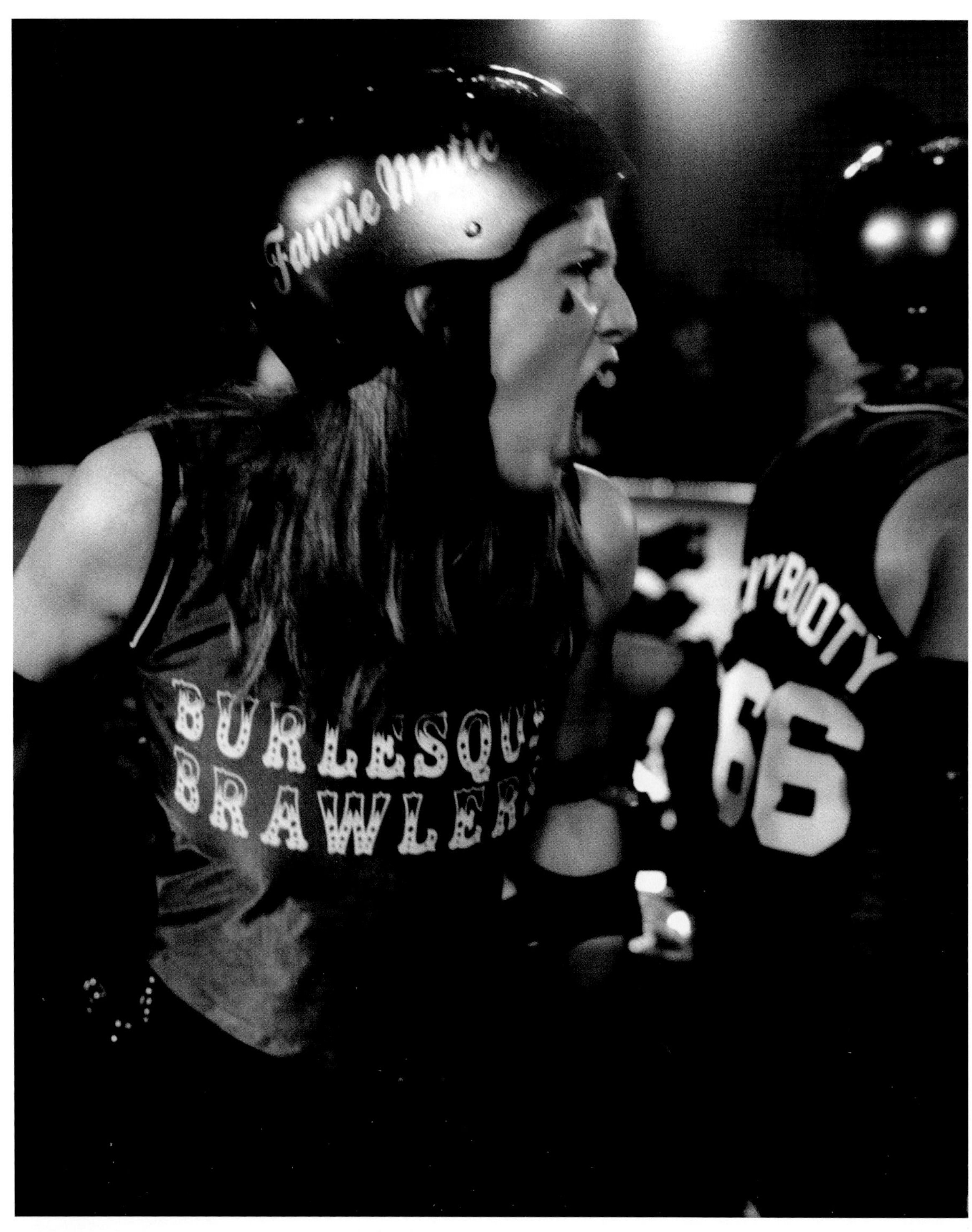

Fannie Matic
BURLESQUE BRAWLERS
BOOTY
66

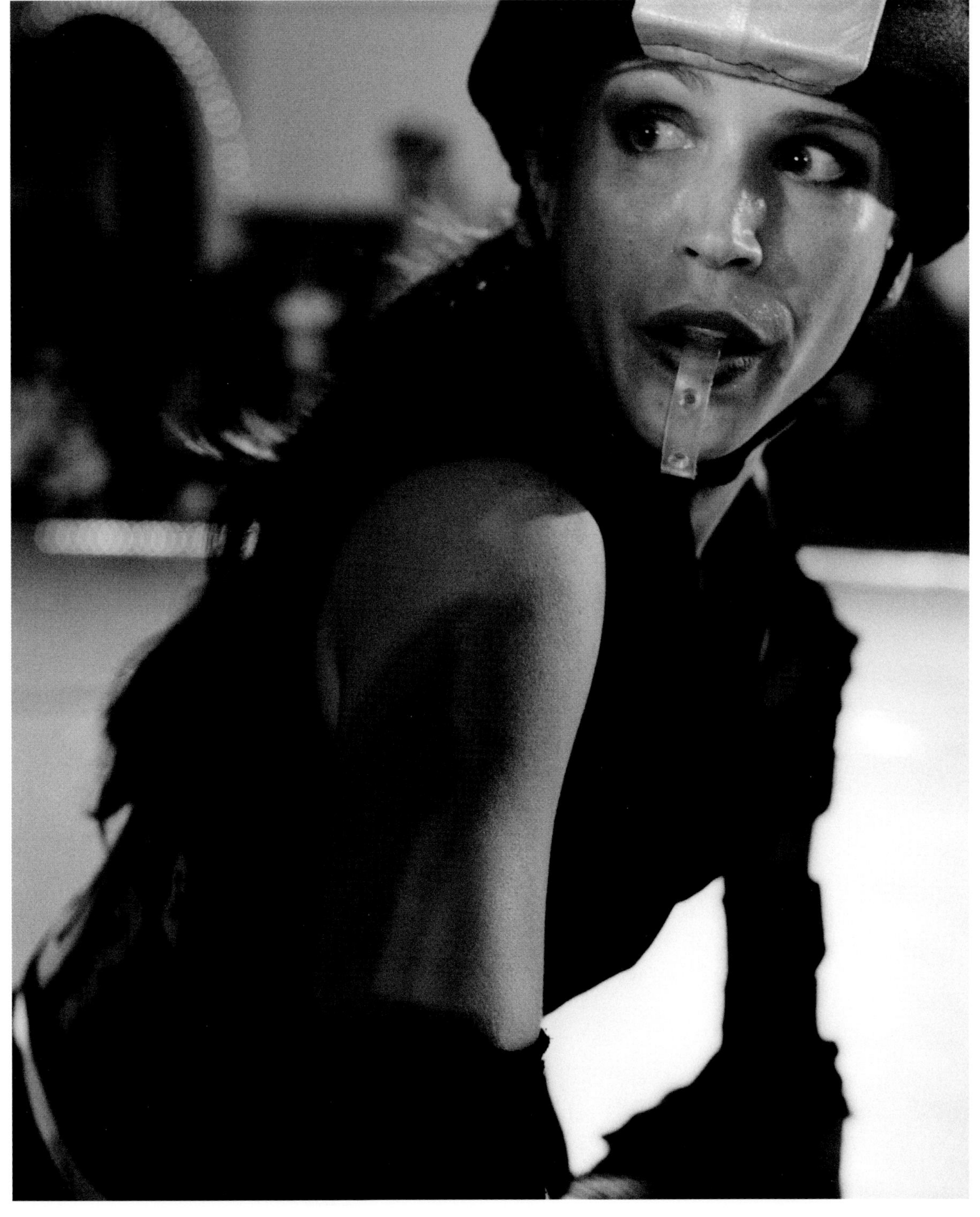

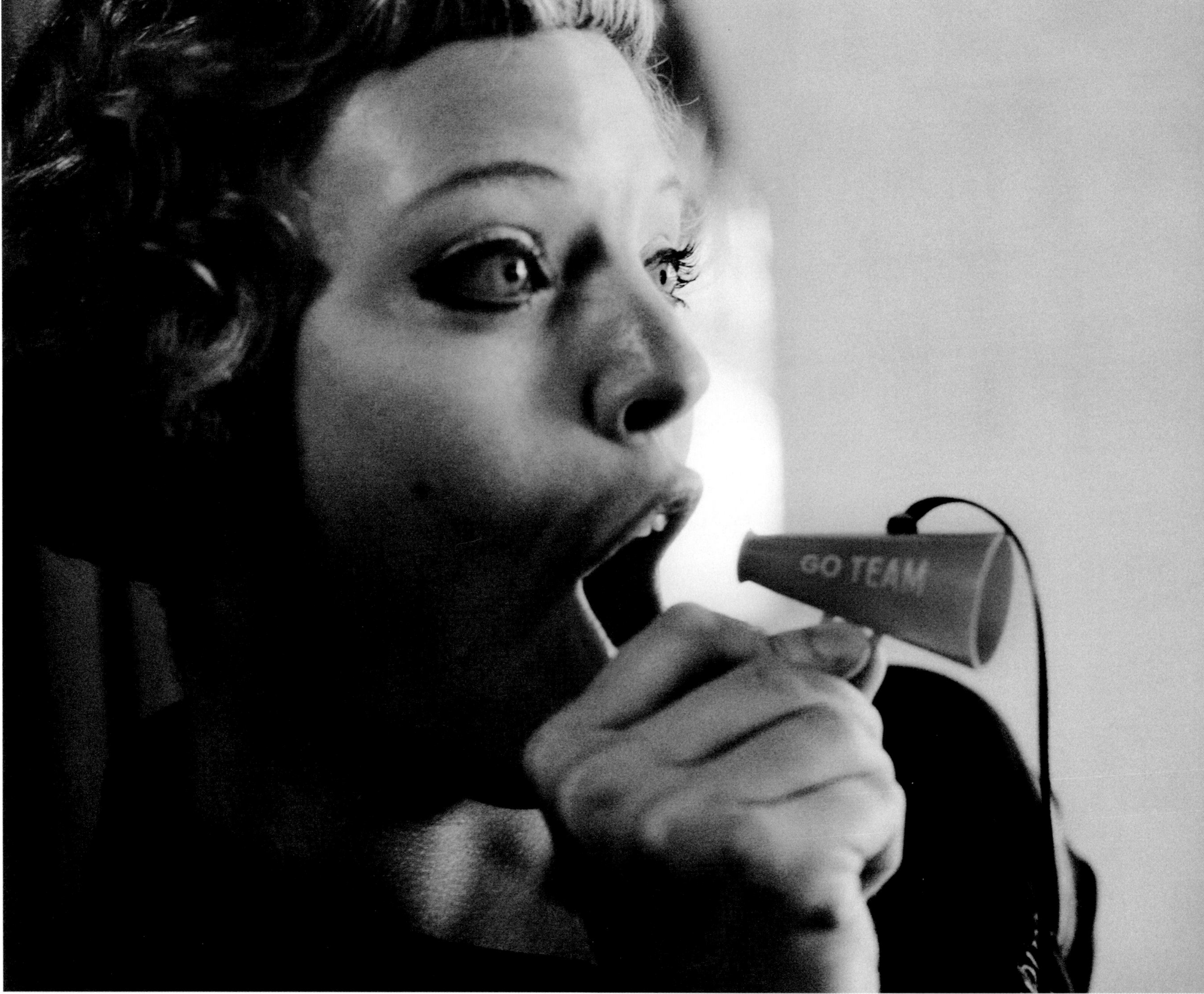
GO TEAM

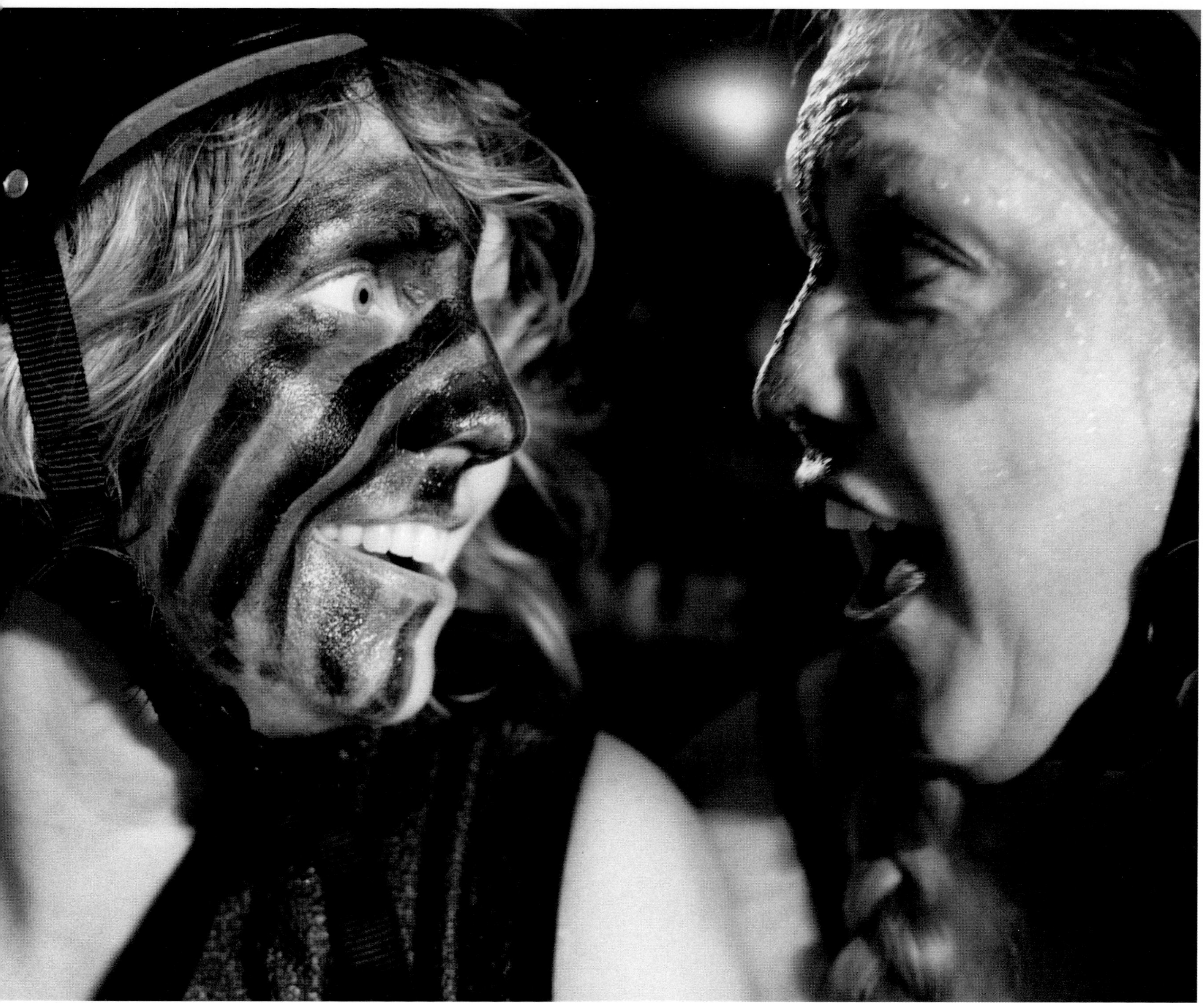

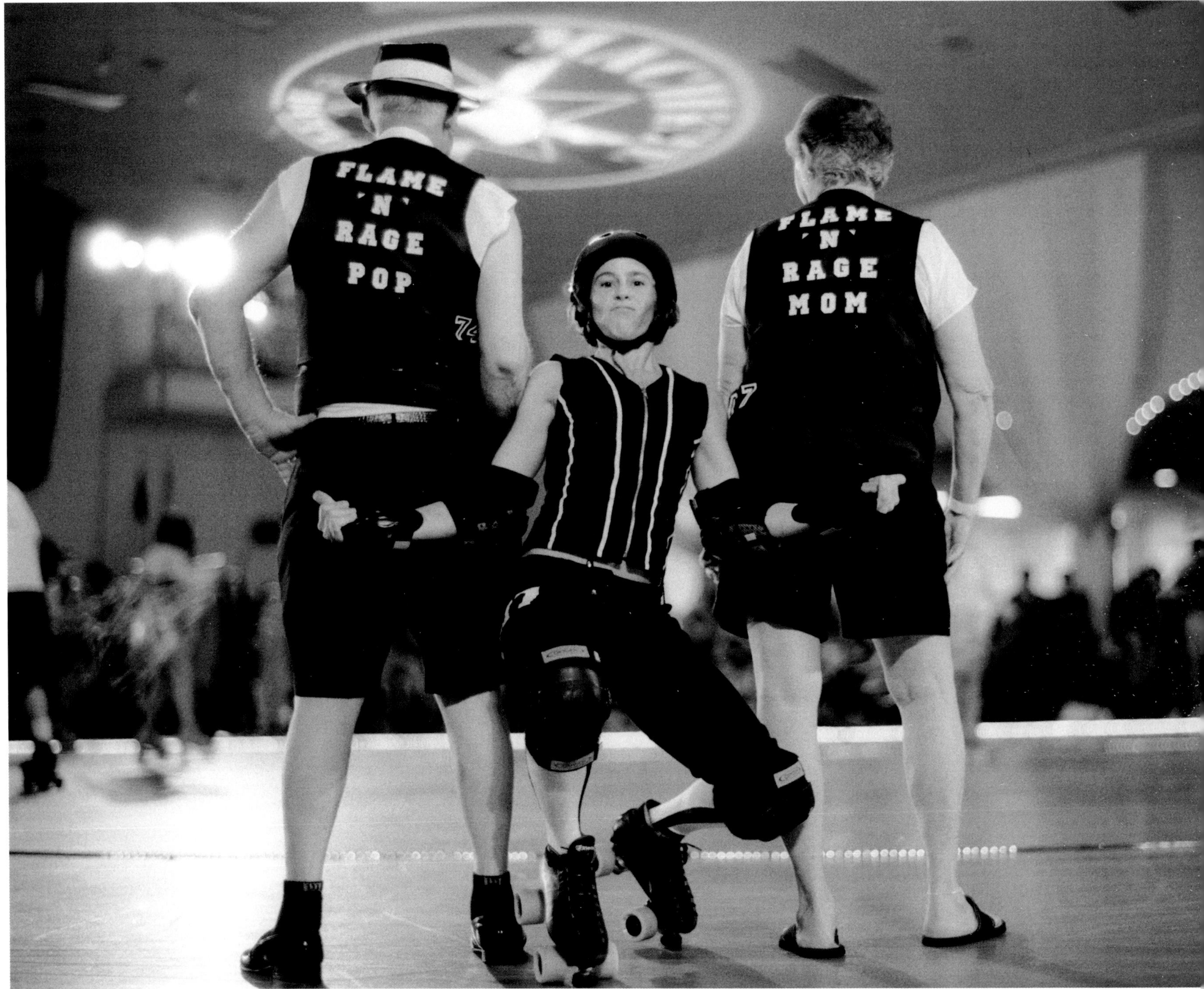
FLAME 'N' RAGE POP
FLAME 'N' RAGE MOM

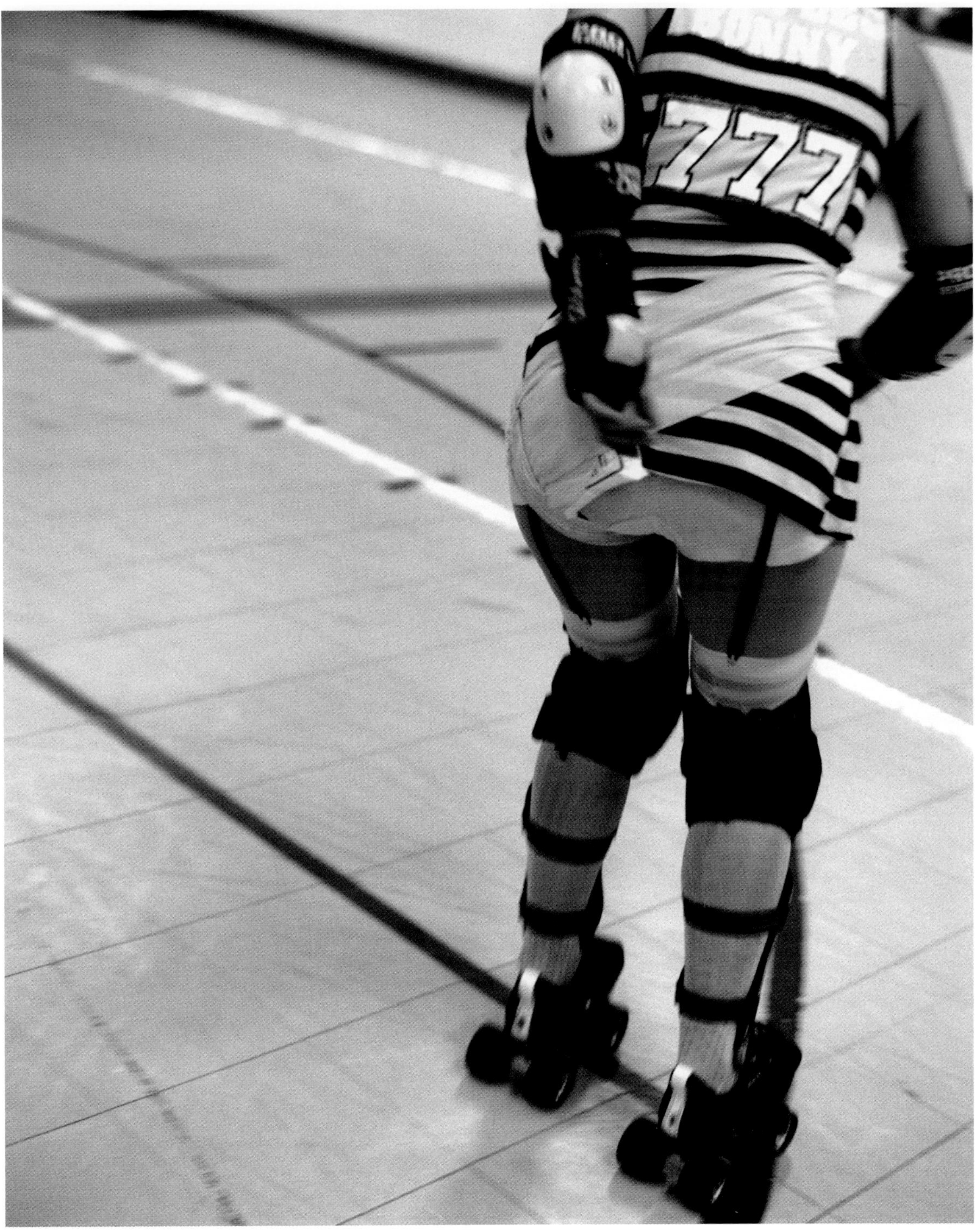

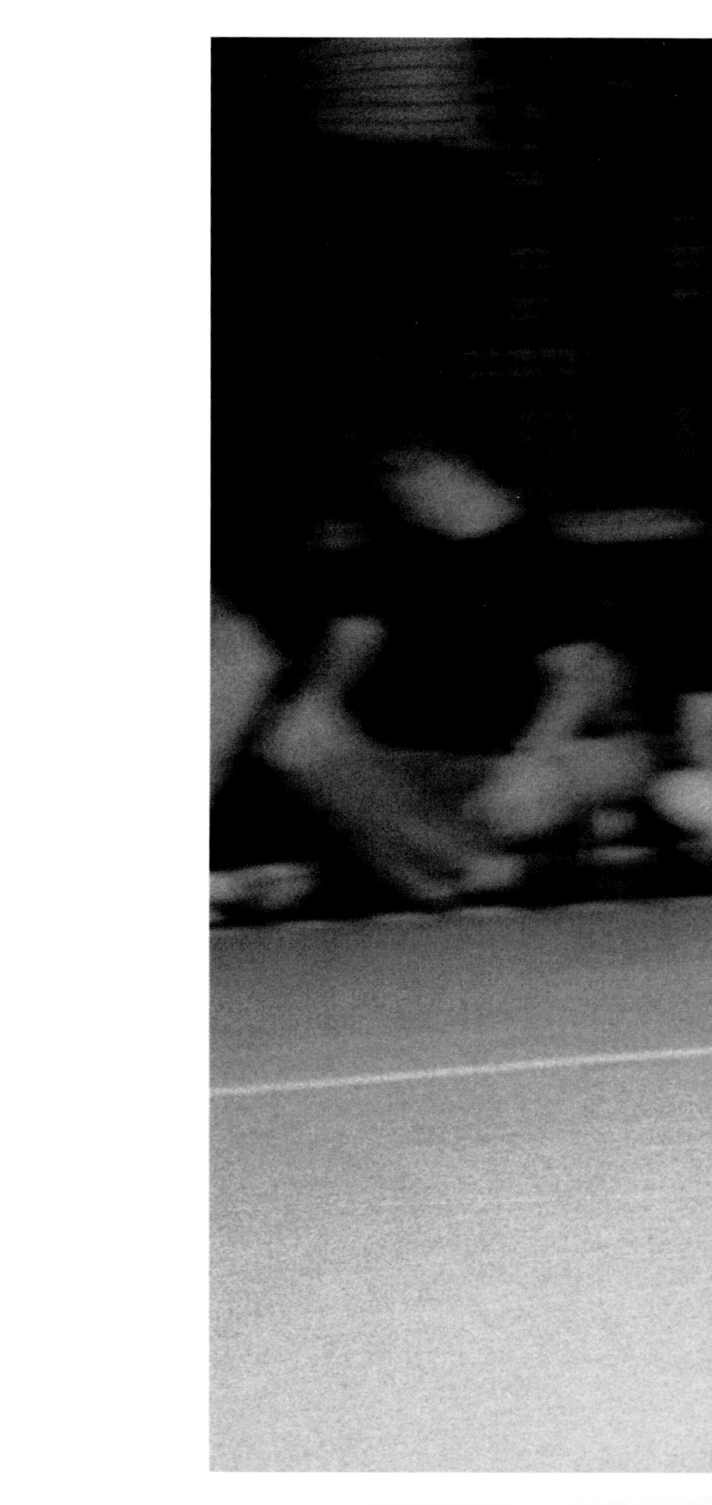

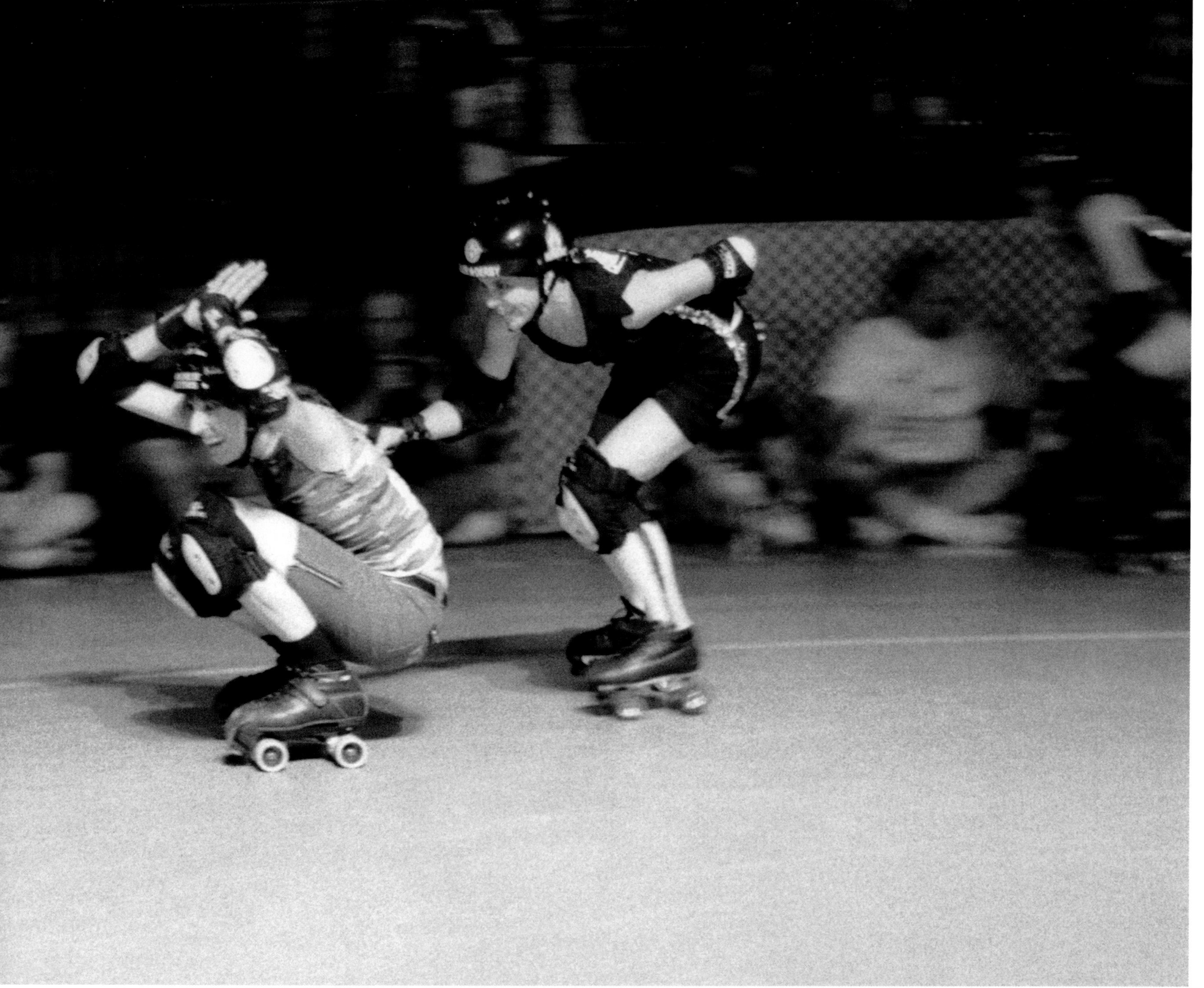

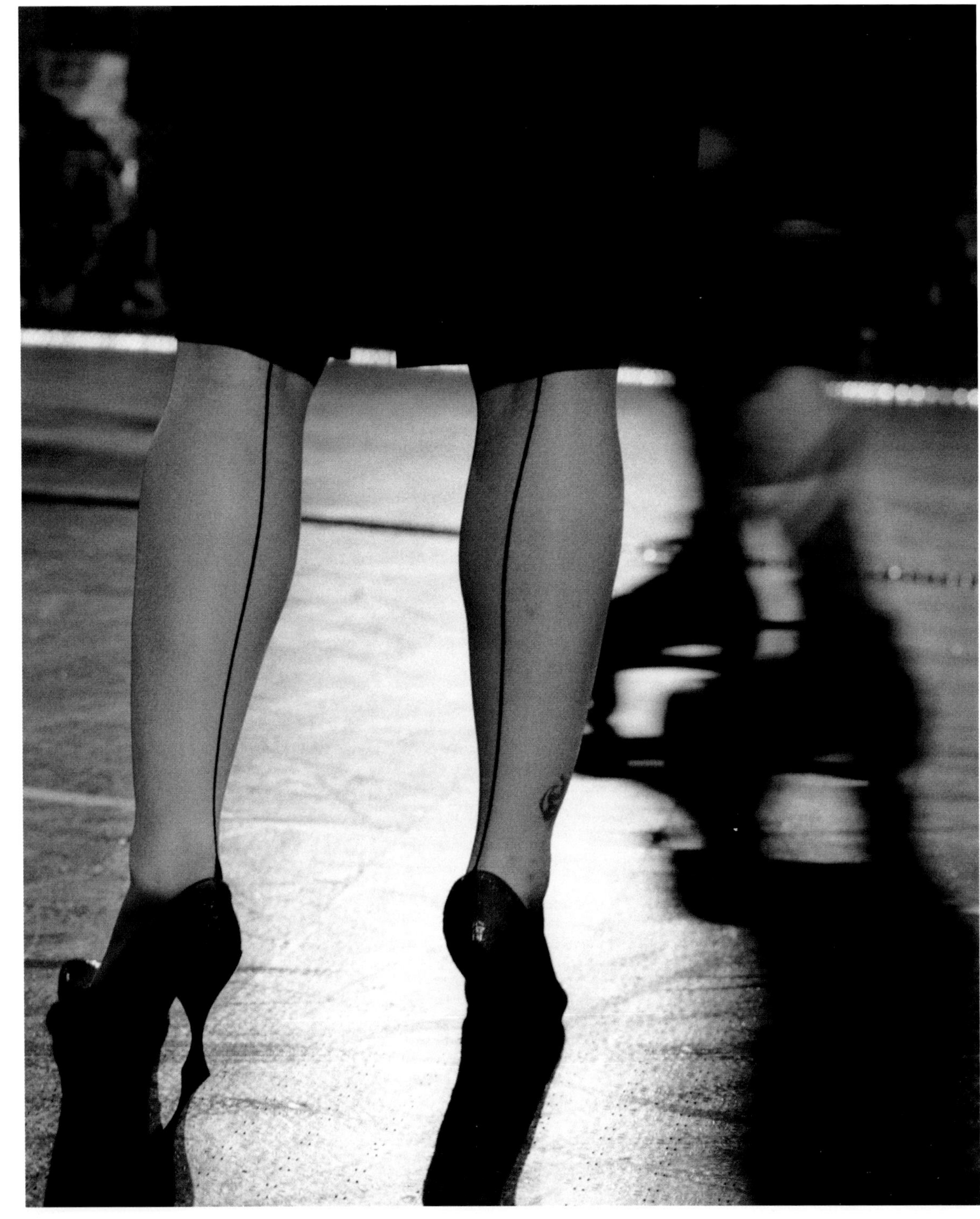

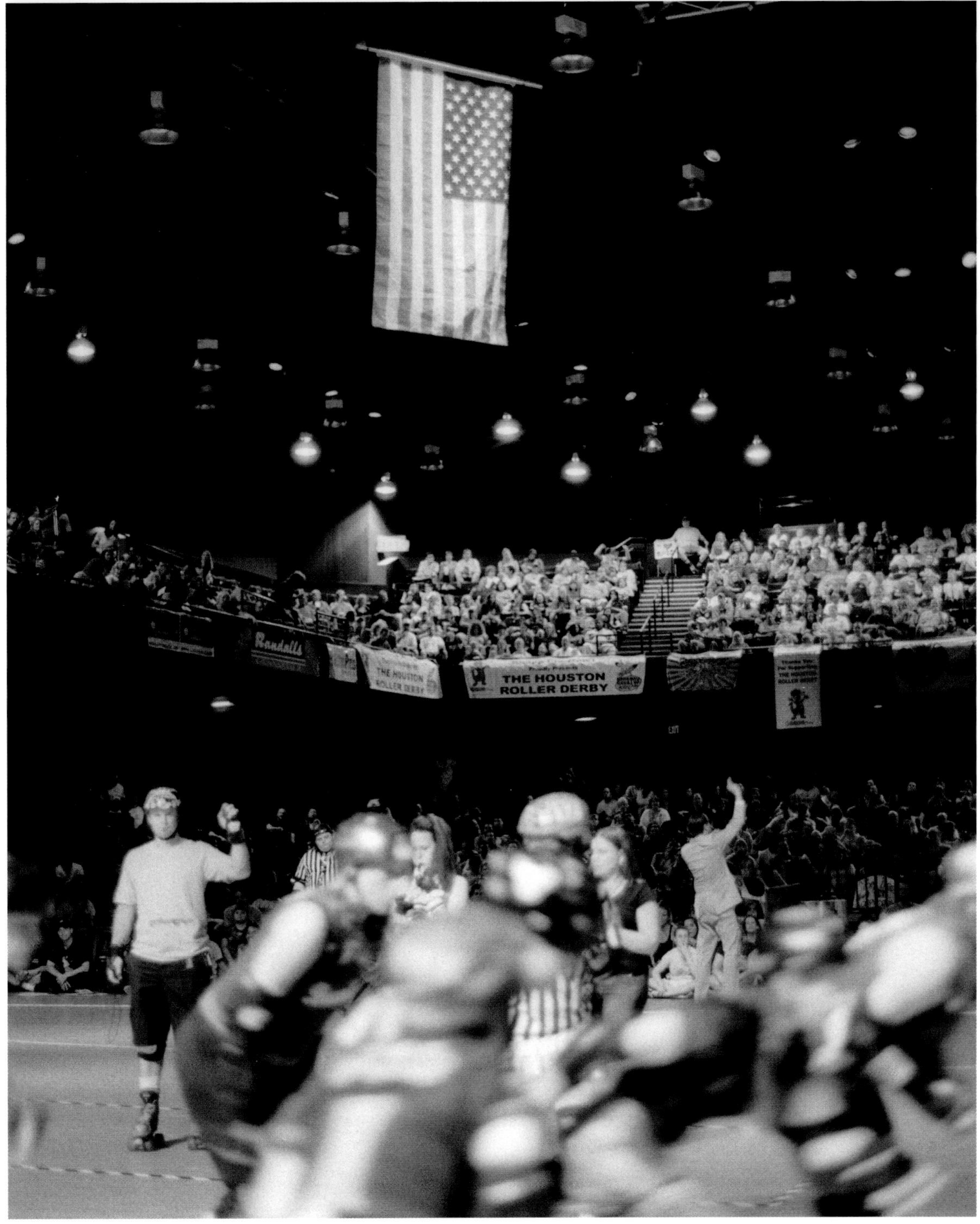
THE HOUSTON
ROLLER DERBY

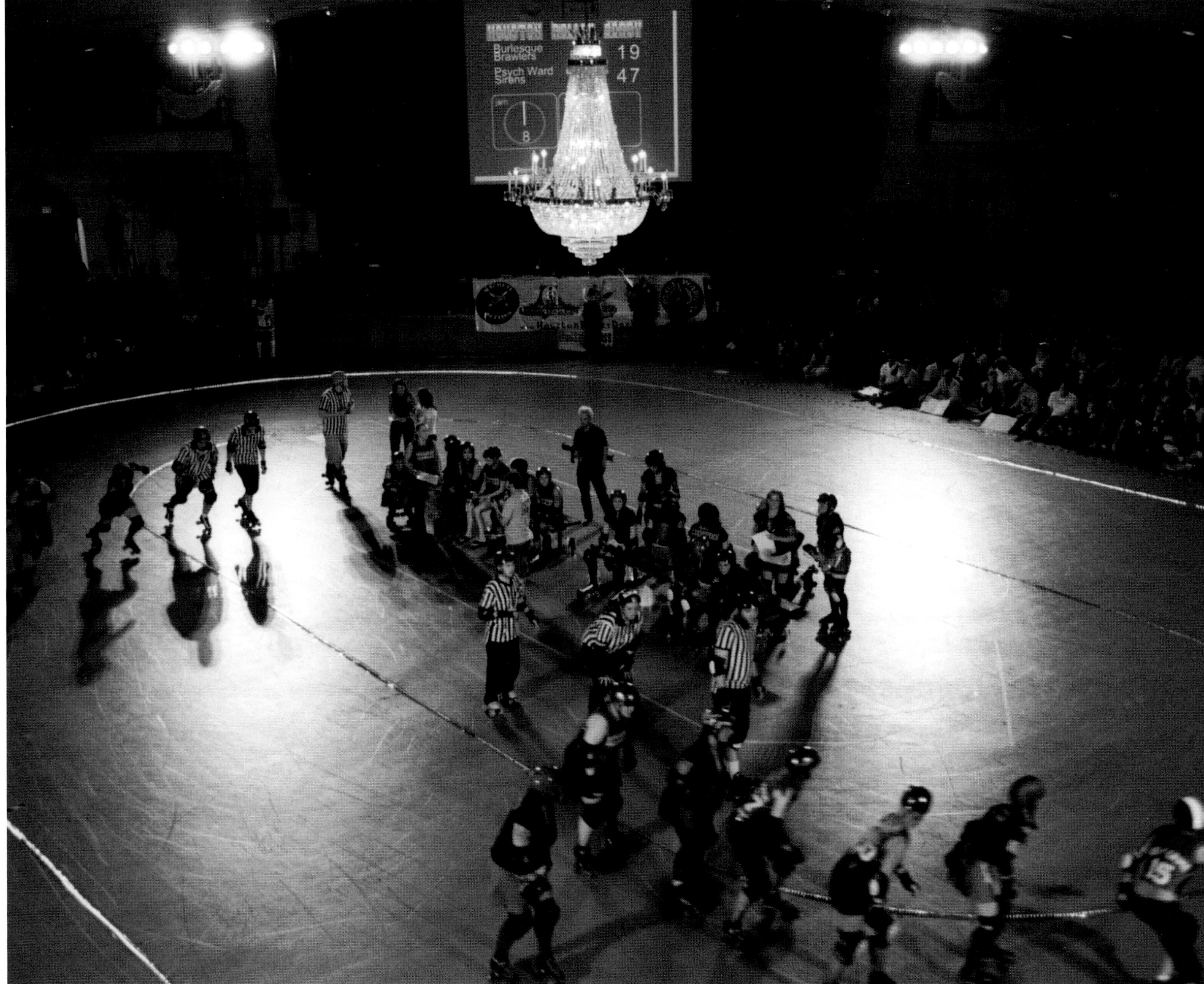

HOUSTON ROLLER DERBY
Burlesque Brawlers   19
Psych Ward Sirens   47
8

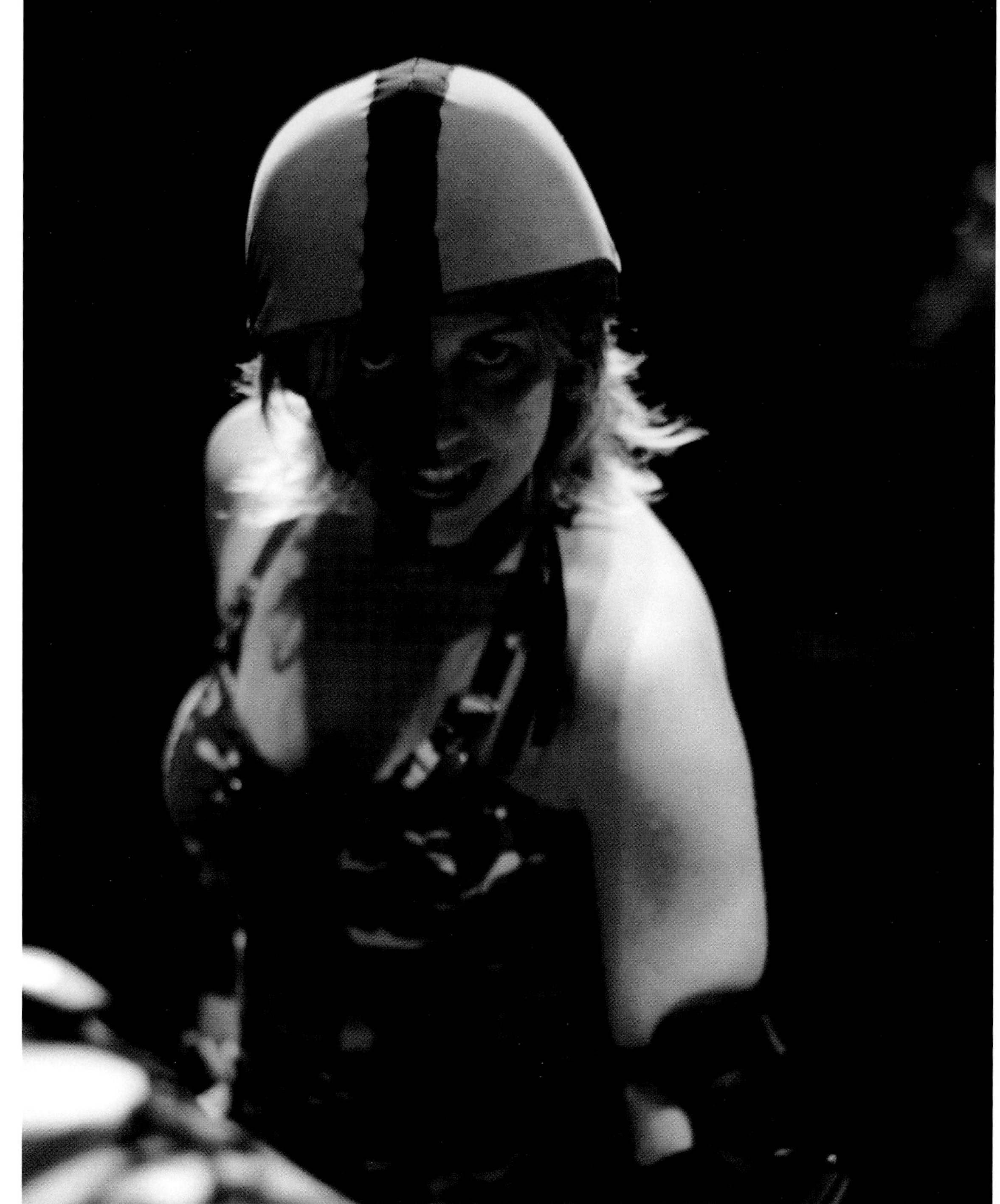

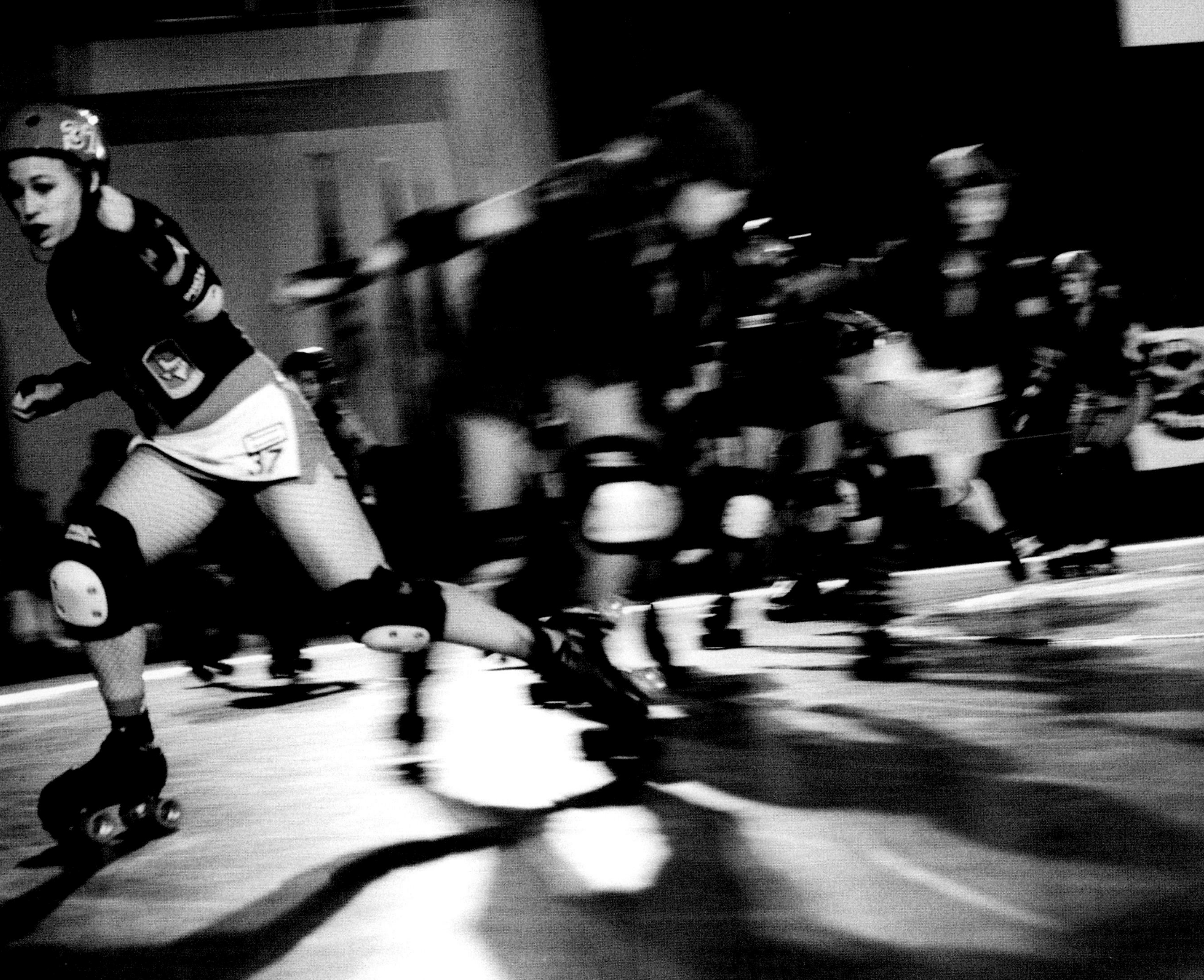

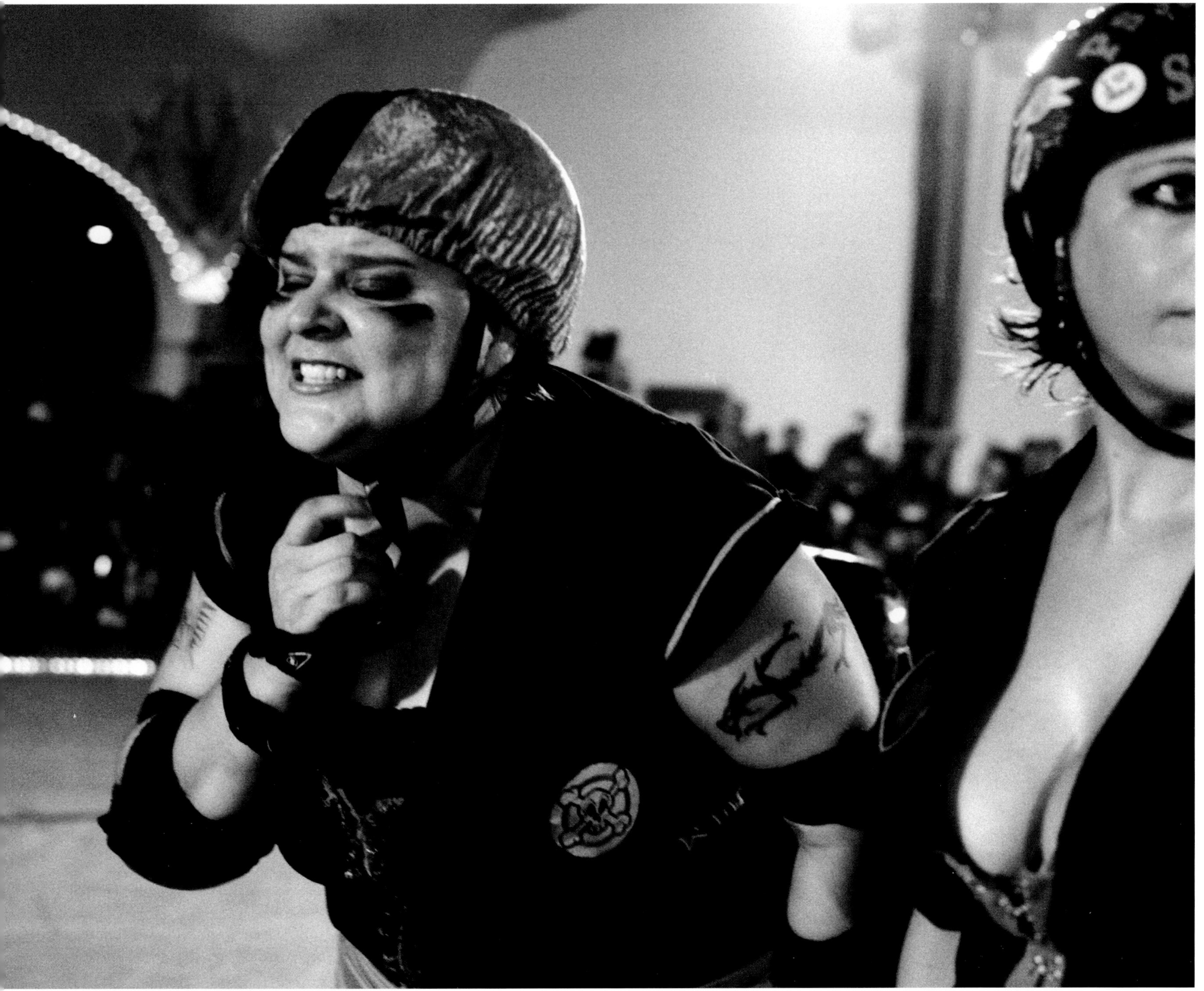

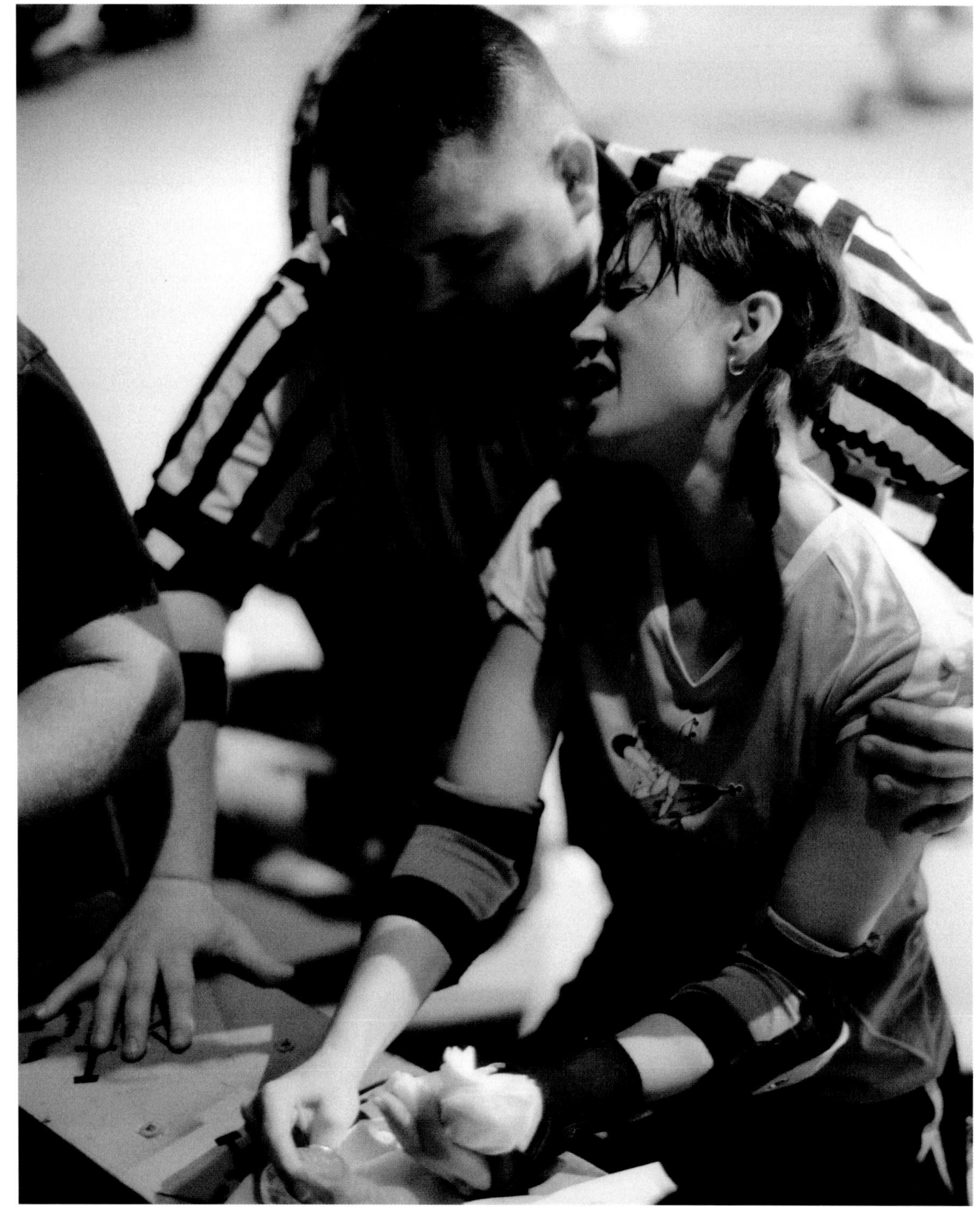

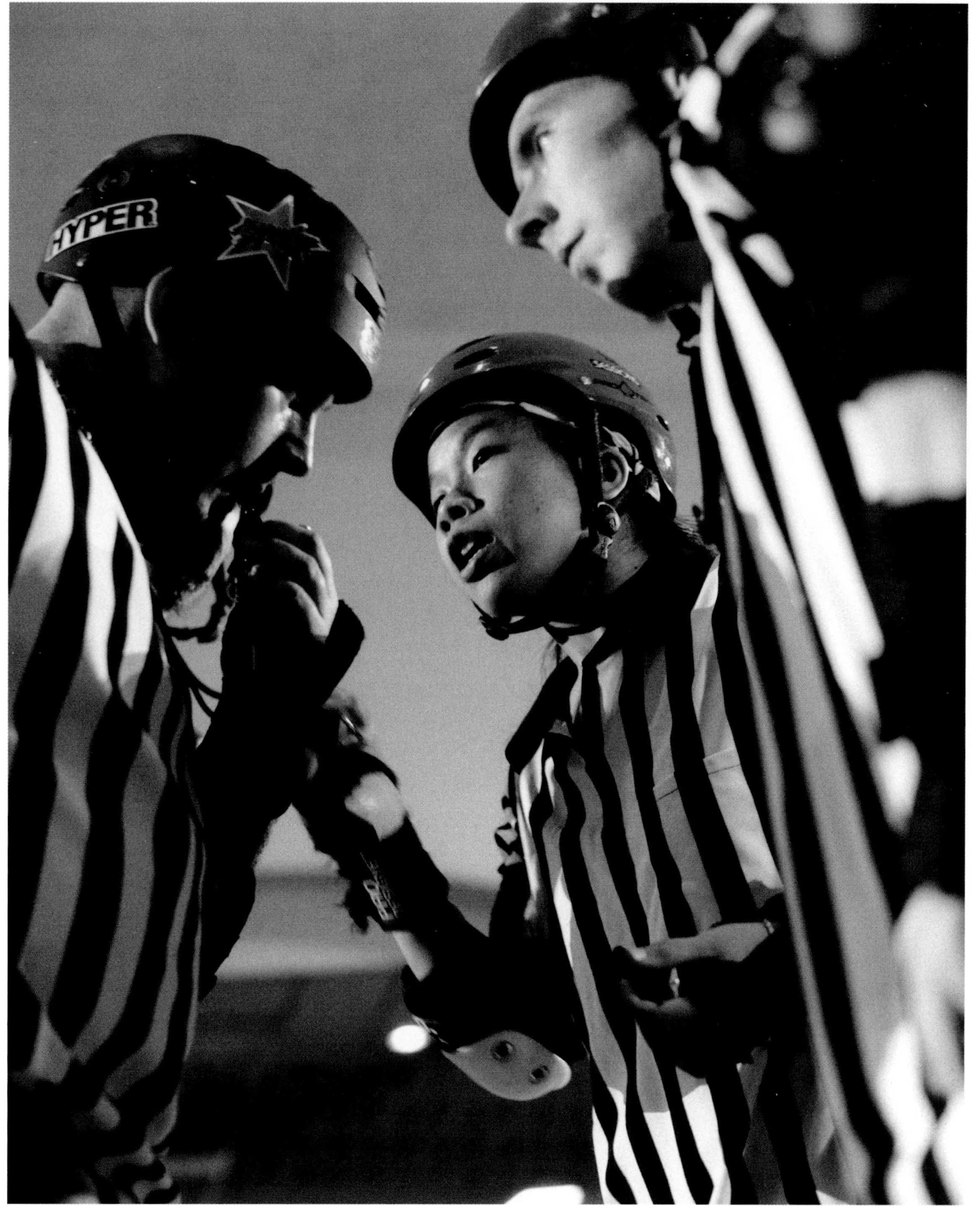

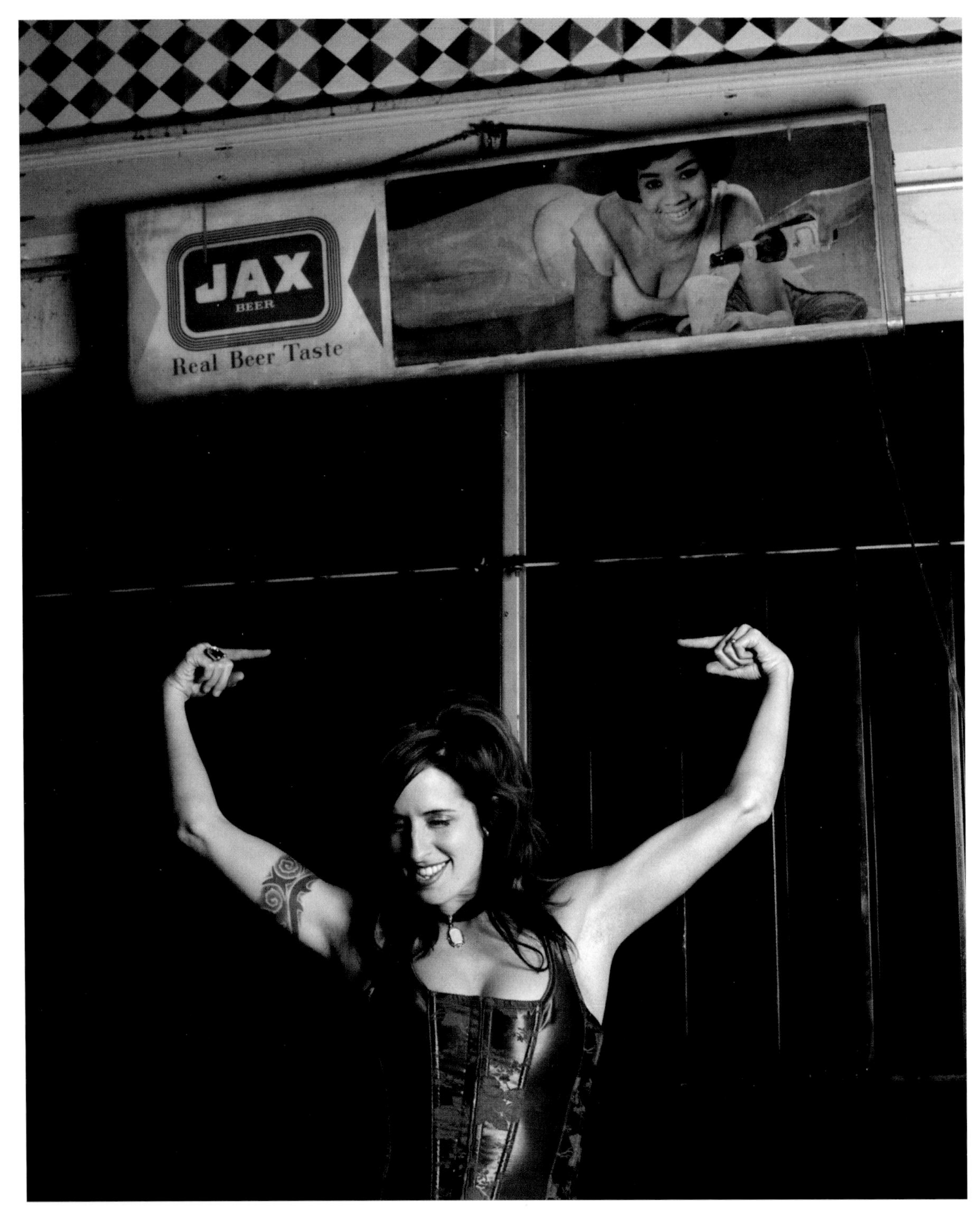
JAX
BEER
Real Beer Taste

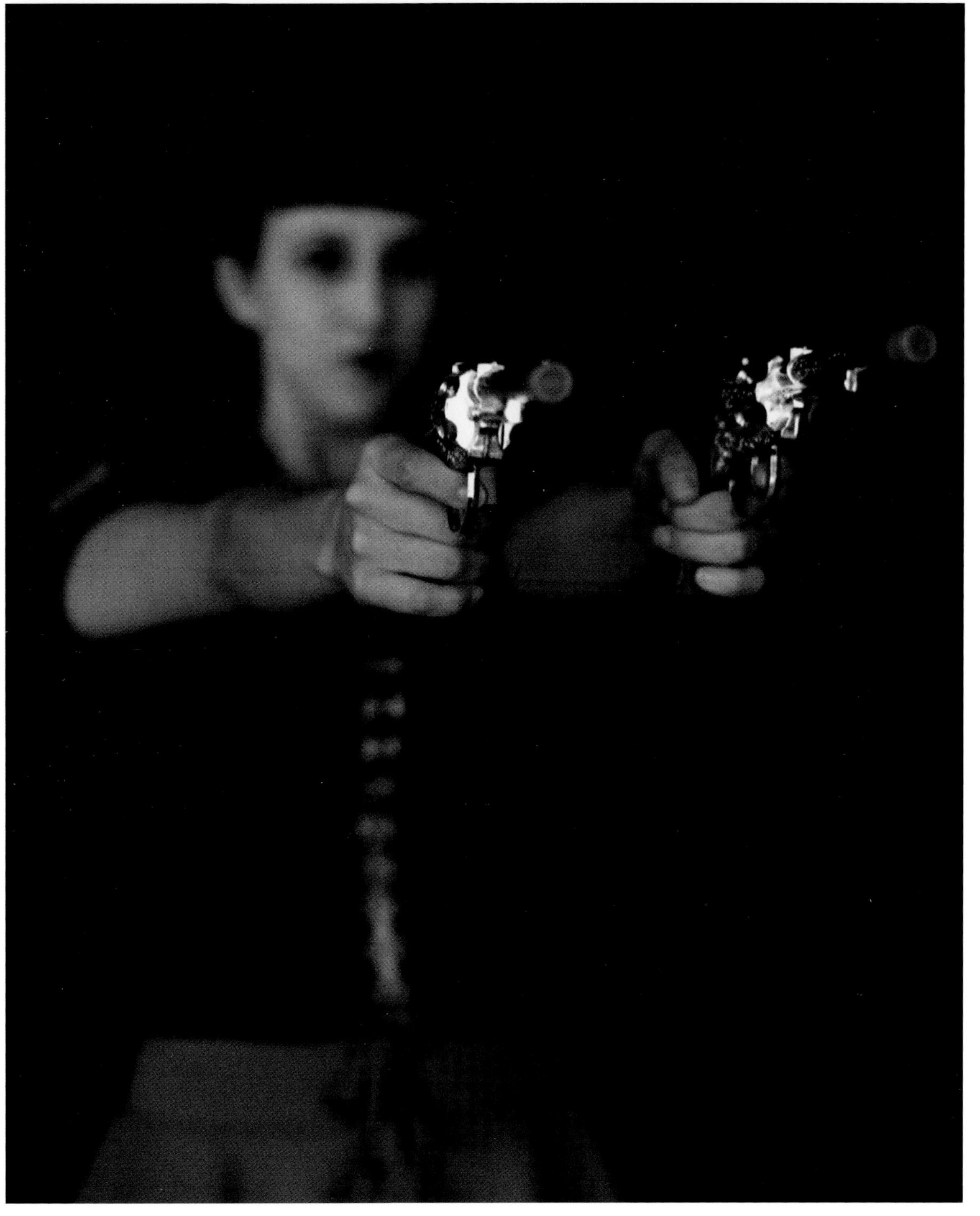

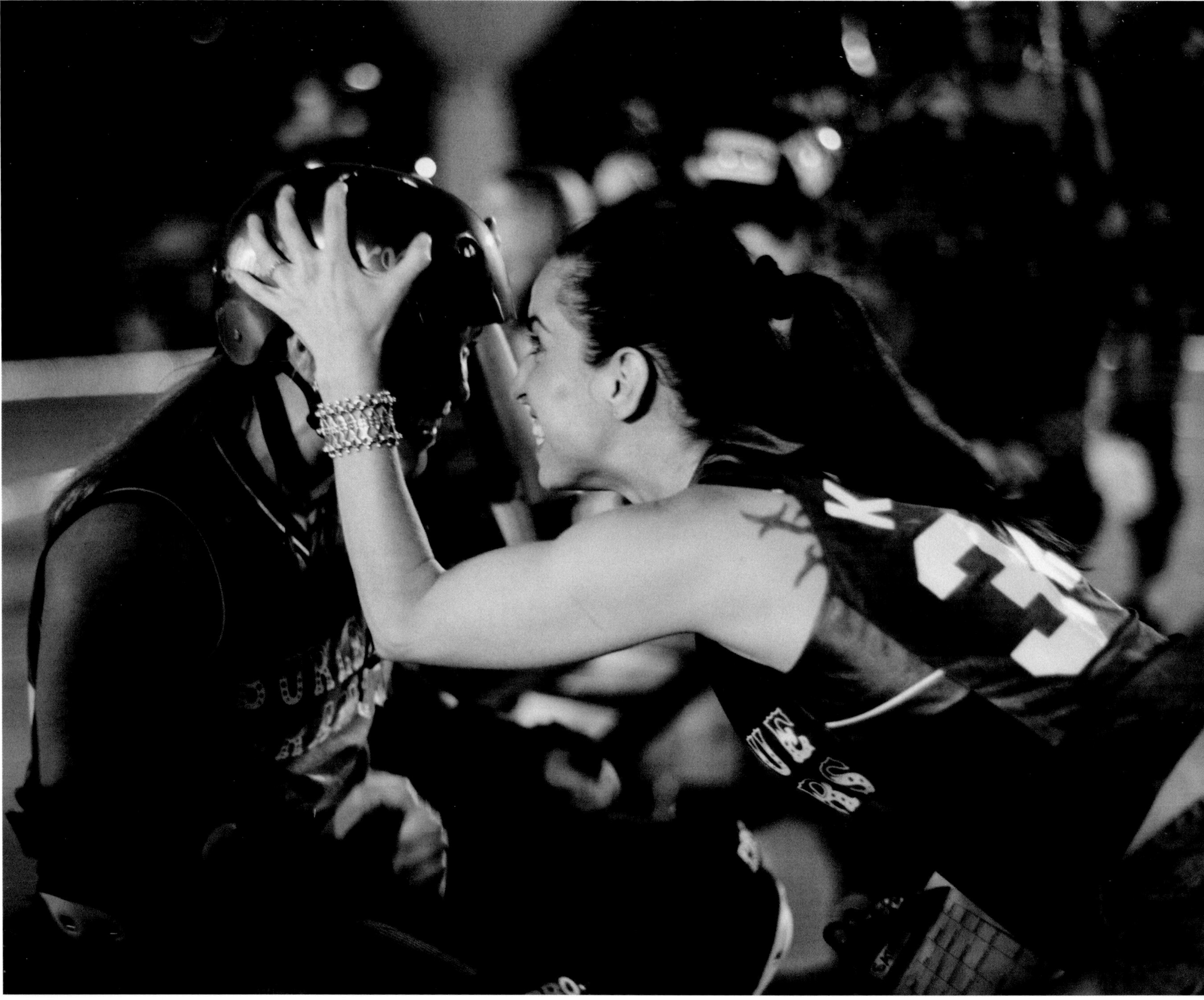

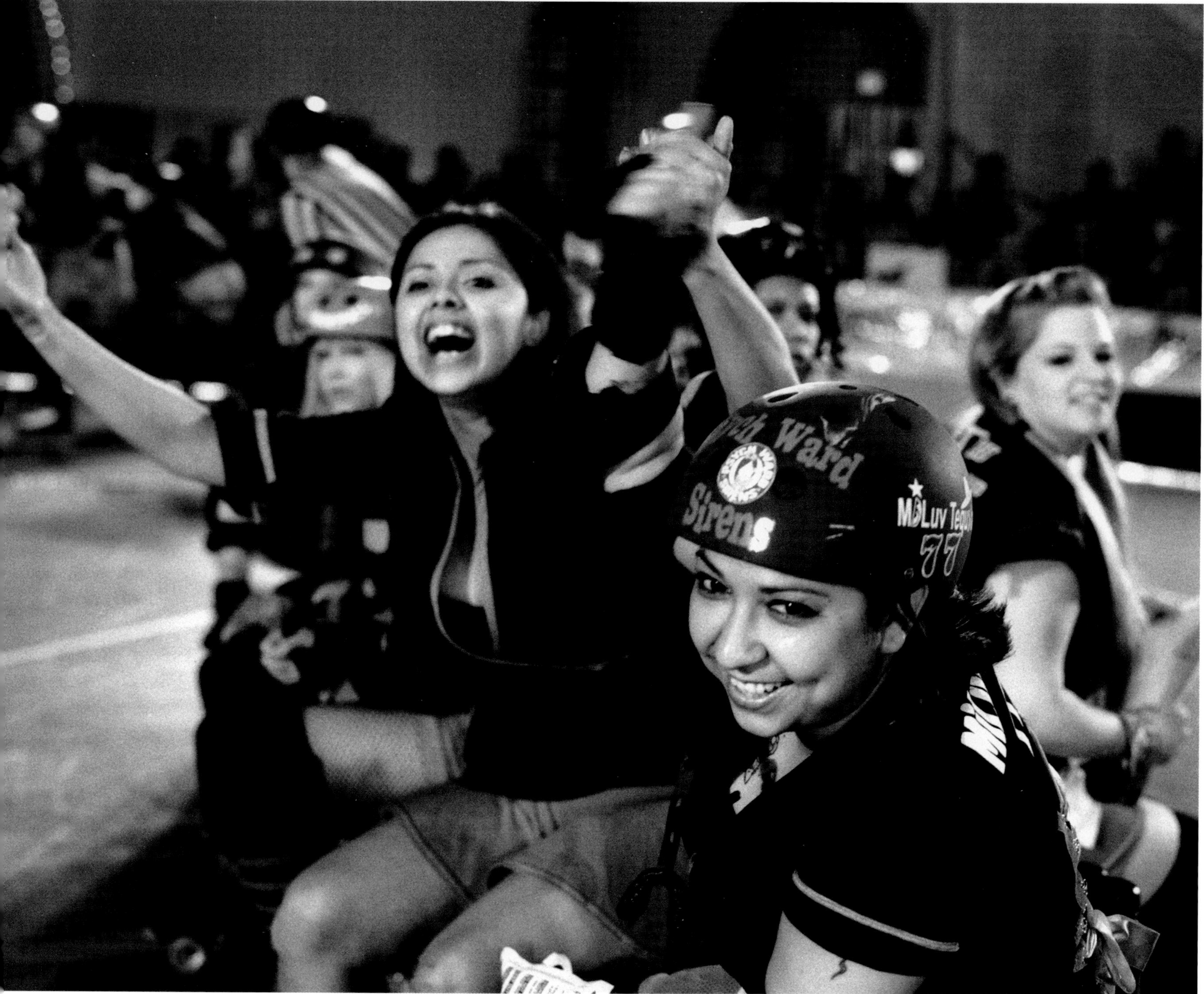

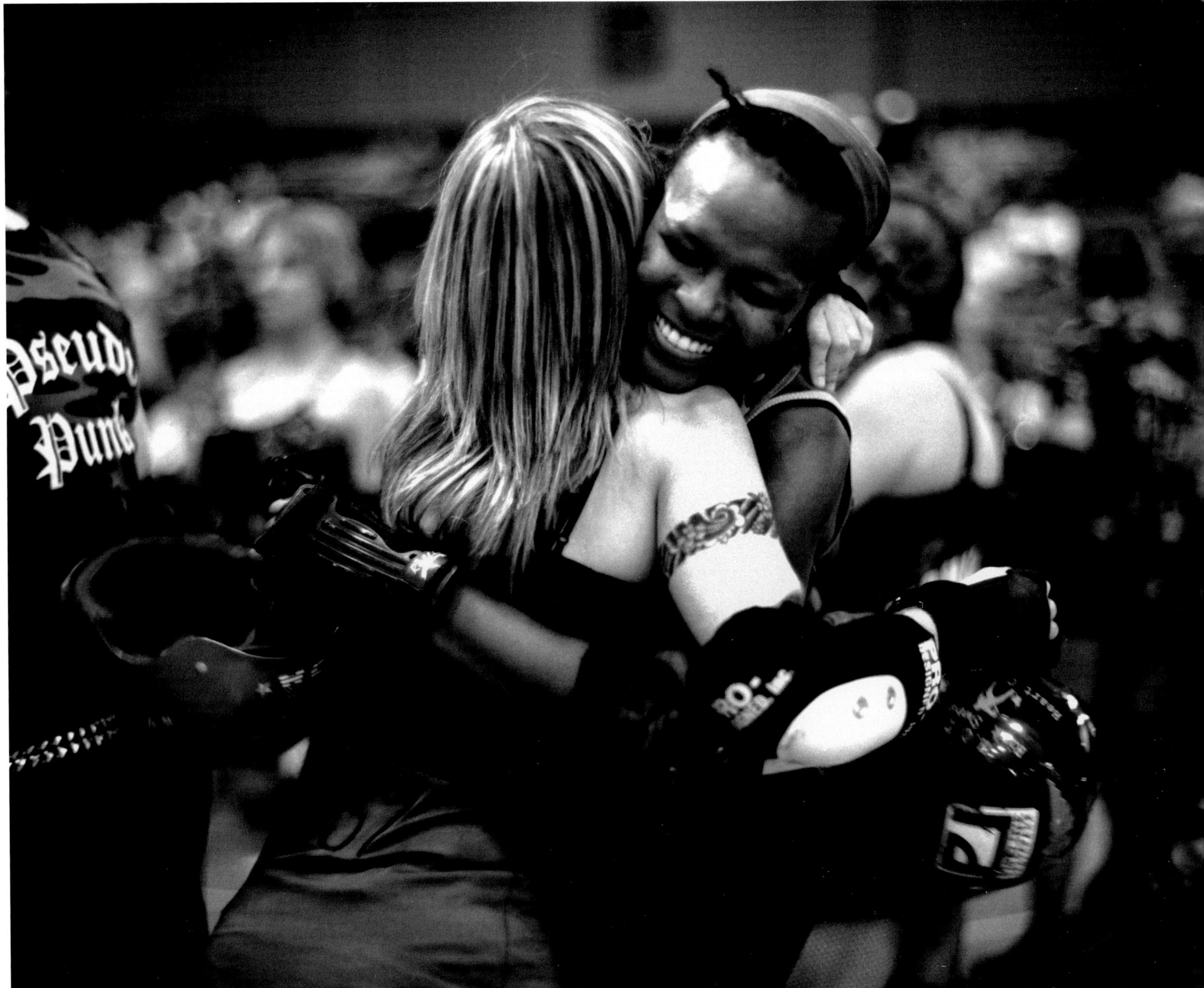
Pseudo
Punc

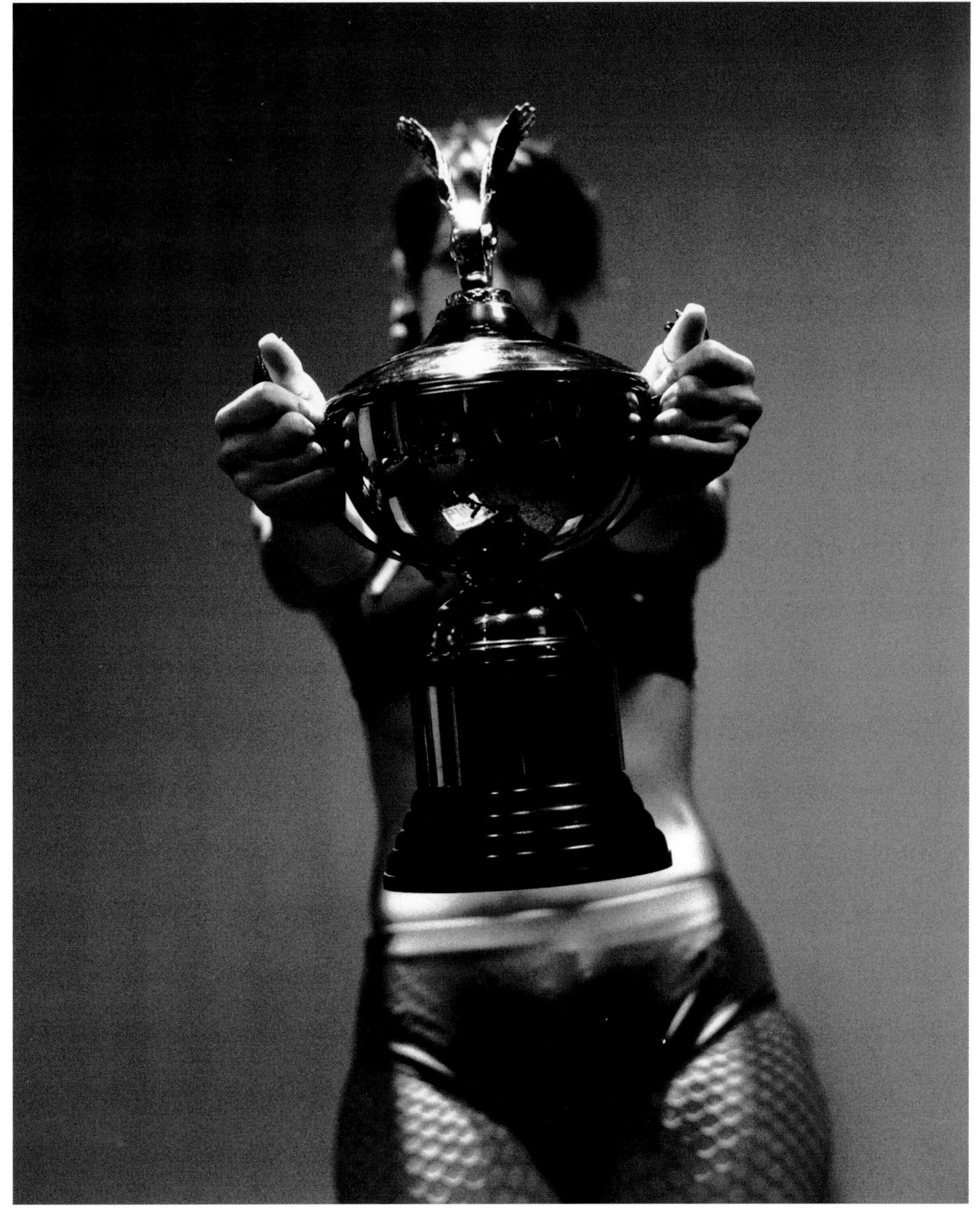

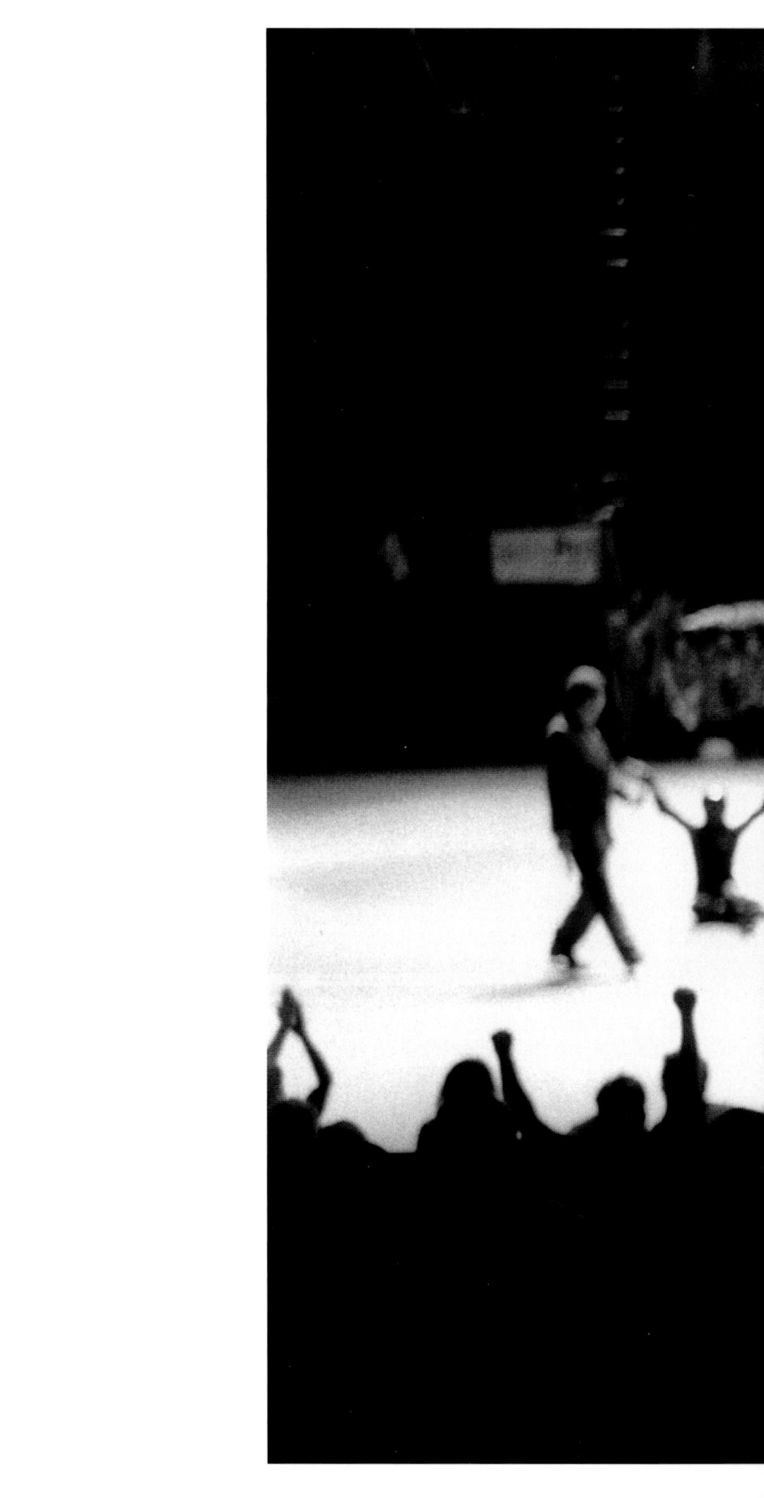

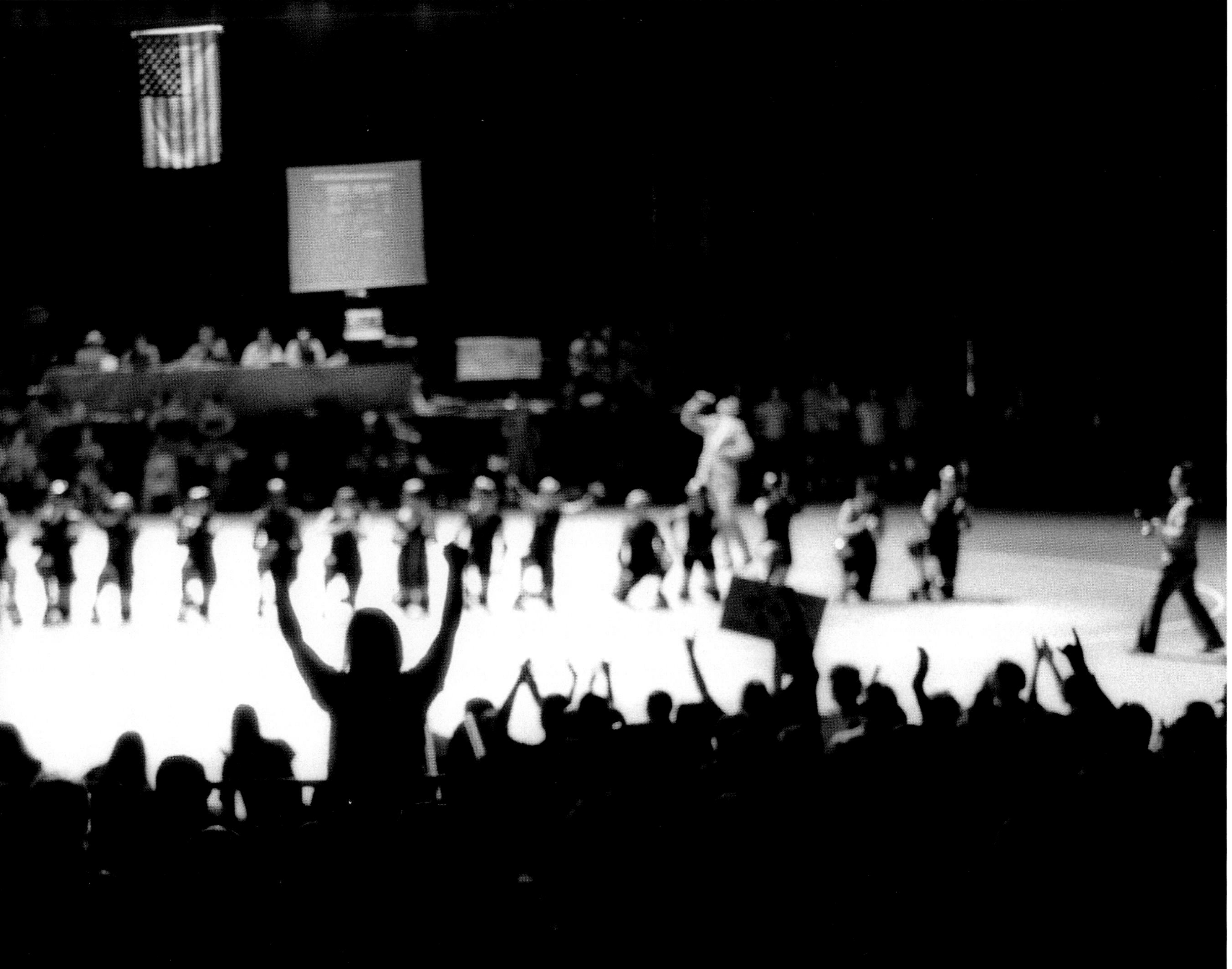

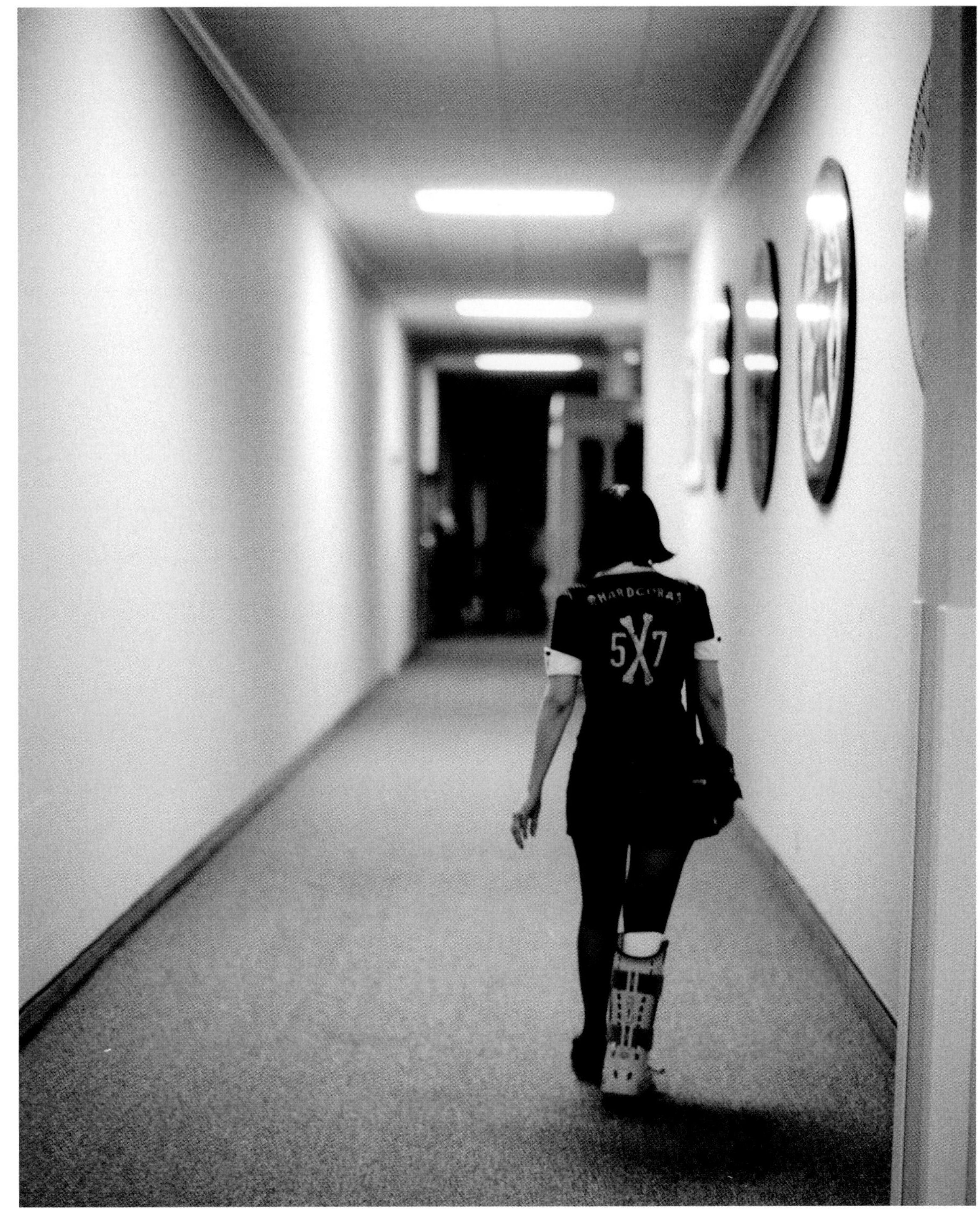

Shelley Calton

BIOGRAPHY
of the Artist

Born in 1959, Houston, Texas. She studied at Sam Houston University and Glassell School of Art as well as under Keith Carter and Debbie Fleming Caffery. Calton is involved in the photography community, serving as board member and auction chairperson for the Houston Center of Photography.

Shelley Calton, Houston 2009

SHOWS
EXHIBITIONS

Group Exhibitions		
	2008	Bering and James
	2007	Watermark Fine Art Photographs and Books
	2005	Heart Gallery Houston/Watermark
	2004	Watermark Fine Art Photographs and Books
	2004	Fotofest/F2

Juried Shows		
	2008	Shots Magazine – Portfolio issue – Cover image
	2008	Women In Photography International – Top Ten Photographs
	2008	Texas Photographic Society – Member Only Show – Honorable Mention
	2008	Pacific Northwest Center for Photography – Plates To Pixels
	2008	Project Basho
	2008	The Photo Review
	2008	Glassell School of Art
	2007	Houston Center for Photography
	2006	The Photo Review
	2006	Houston Center for Photography
	2005	Houston Center for Photography
	2004	The Photo Review
	2004	Houston Center for Photography
	2003	Bosque Conservatory
	2003	Houston Center for Photography

HARD KNOCKS

Image Titles

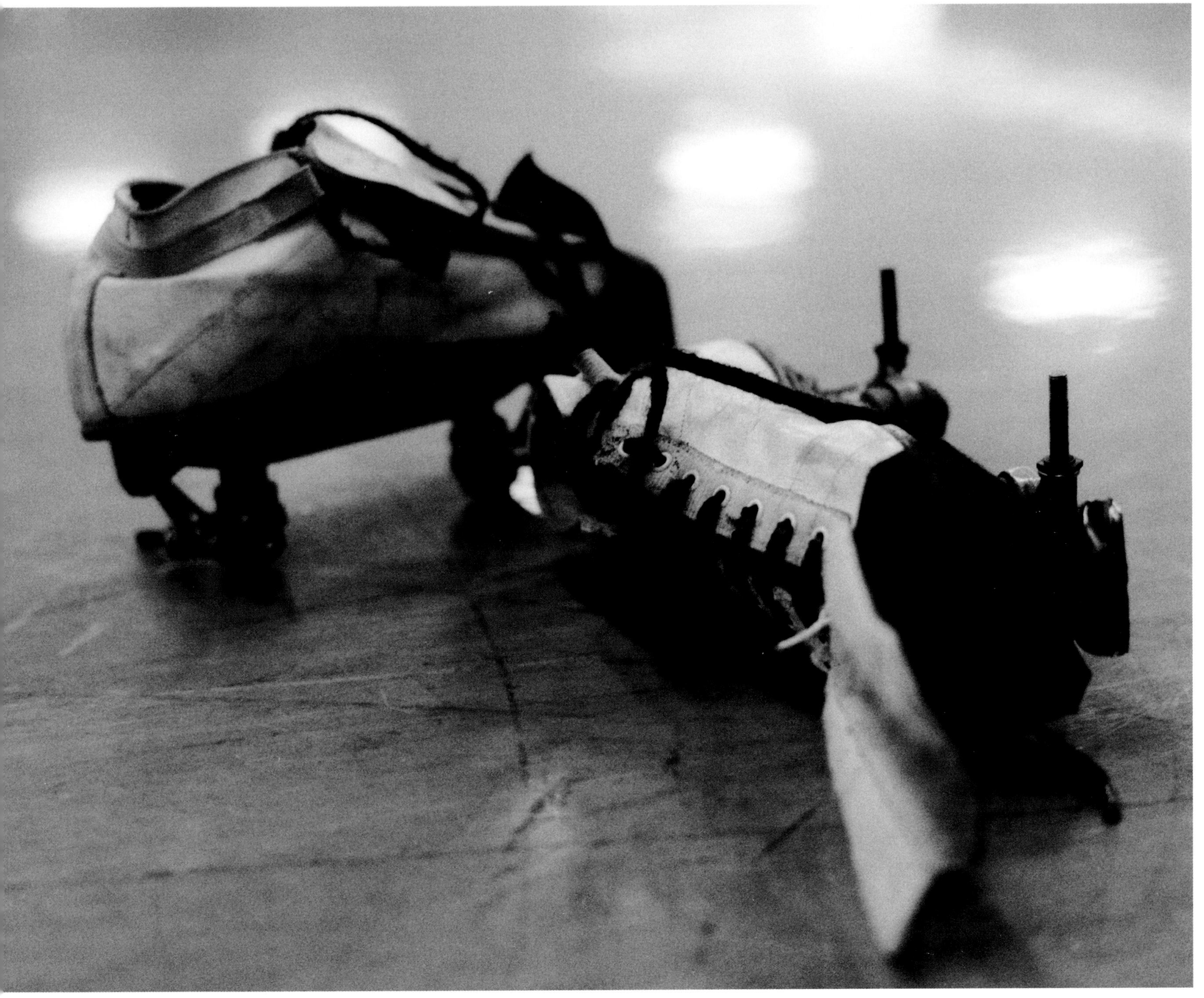

IM PRINT

Rolling with the Derby Girls

© 2009 Kehrer Verlag Heidelberg,
Shelley Calton and Tracy Xavia Karner

Texts: Shelley Calton and Tracy Xavia Karner

Design: Kehrer Design Heidelberg (Leslie Jean Stuart)

Proofreading: Kehrer Design Heidelberg (Tom Grace)

Image processing: Kehrer Design Heidelberg
(Jürgen Hofmann, René Henoch)

Printed in Germany

Bibliographic information published by the
Deutsche Nationalbibliothek:
The Deutsche Nationalbibliothek lists this publication in
the Deutsche Nationalbibliografie; detailed bibliographic
data are available in the Internet at http://dnb.d-nb.de.

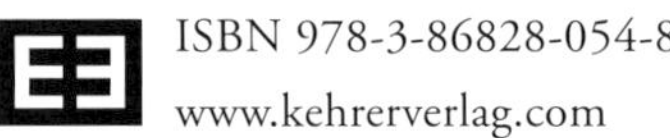

ISBN 978-3-86828-054-8
www.kehrerverlag.com